Kundalini
and the Secrets of Silence

Jeremy Vaeni

Kynegion House

Kynegion House

Front Cover Design: John Randall
Printed in USA

"We are lived by powers we pretend to understand"

In Memory of Ernst Toller, W.H. Auden

Caramel & White

A single house fly made home on her back and I knew she was over. Caramel & White floated in the shallow blue kiddie pool, dying but not dead. Sicker than she had been yesterday, for sure. Unable to walk and happy, if that's the word—and it isn't—happy to be off her palmate feet. The weight of life was too much to bear for much longer. Her buoyancy on the water helped with that. She still had the unending warmth of the Hawaiian sun and she had family. That was enough for now.

Her flock wandered over grass just outside the electrified poultry netting that formed the circumference of their duck run. I was careful not to let them in lest they steal her water or her food. They were doing just fine with seeds and insects, which populated the freshly turned earth that wild pigs had rooted through the night before. From across the fence they were good company.

Yesterday, Caramel & White ached to be with them. Today, she made due with facing in their direction from the waters where she was too weak and too tired to escape. Ordinarily, if she were cut off from them by the poultry netting, she would pace with them from her side. If they walked out of eyeshot she would honk for them to come back. There would be no honking today.

Caramel & White is a beautiful duck, so named for her mostly caramel-colored feathering with the slightest triangle of white on her neck. She is one of eight: seven females and one male. One glorious, colorful male—a welsh harlequin cleverly named *Welsh Harlequin*. He surely would have had his way with her if it weren't for this lousy fencing.

Or would he have?

Maybe not today.

I

FOWL MYTHS

"First of all, if you really want to discuss it, have a dialogue about it, would you forget everything you have heard about it? Would you? We are entering into a subject which is very serious. It isn't just an amusement for a morning. Are you willing to forget everything that you have felt about it, what your gurus have told about it, or your attempt to awaken it, and start with a carte blanche. You know what a carte blanche is: a completely clean slate. Can you?"

- Explorations and Insights, Jiddu Krishnamurti

Introducktion
Ducking Around

It was a warm Fall day in New York City. Not at all muggy. Perfect weather for lunch in Central Park. My low-level job of smiling at one-percenters from behind a receptionist's desk afforded me only one half-hour break, but I always made the best of it by staring at the large duckpond from a park bench at 5th Avenue and 59th Street. It was here that I once witnessed the greatest bit of natural trolling I'd ever seen: a massive goose flying into the pond aimed for, and dropped squarely upon, the head of an unsuspecting lone duck. The duck plunged into the drink and popped back up a few feet away. She shook it off, looking this way and that as if to say, "Well, I never!" and swam off quickly, muttering under her breath the incivility of it all. The goose looked around in mock innocence like a smirking bully rhetorically asking, "What?"

This day, however, I chose not to sit on my favorite bench. I found a nice private spot on a rock beyond some shrubbery to sit at pond's edge, undisturbed. As I gazed at the calm waters in this manmade nature haven, a line of ducks, six or seven of them, swam into my sightline coming from my right to my left. When they were lined up directly in front of me they all stopped at once. They behaved like one being in many bodies. Starting from the lead swimmer on, one by one they turned and faced me.

Silently they sat. Bobbing.

Silently I sat. Not bobbing.

It was eerie. It felt supernatural. I thought they were conveying a message to me, but I couldn't tell what. Probably that I was on their favorite rock and I should go —but it felt like more than that at the time because of their perfectly mechanical behavior and the way they seemed to be assessing me, waiting for me to make a move.

I got up and left more than a little weirded out. Some sort of trickster entity must have gotten ahold of these ducks to let me know that I was being watched by invisible forces just at the tip of my comprehension. Of this I had little doubt, for I lived a life where far stranger things had occurred. We call such things *paranormal* or *alien*. *High strangeness experiences*. But at some point we have to ask ourselves why we otherize events that are woven into the fabric of our lives. Events that often shape us.

I wasn't asking that back in Central Park. No, back there I added to my high strangeness list, Ducks Behaving As If Possessed By A Single Intelligence To Convey Some Riddle To Me. It is not lost on me that a list this self-centered could easily be a checklist of delusions of grandeur, except most of the time the experiences don't feel grand. They feel somewhere between confusing and terrifying. At least initially this was the case. It got better with time.

These ducks forming a kickline while staring me down were, by this point in my life, a mere creepy curiosity that I could babble about to my best friend and podcasting partner, Jeff Ritzmann, on our *Paratopia* show. Nothing too scary there.

Cut to 20 years later when my newlywed wife, Carol, and I bought and raised eight ducks at our home in

Hawaii. Ducks, I found out, sometimes perform militarized choreography like what happened in Central Park that day, turning one at a time down the line to stare at you. Once, and never again to my knowledge, they sat in a perfect circle facing outward on the front lawn. Ducks do these things naturally. They often walk single file, too. I hadn't given much thought to the old adage, "Get all your ducks in a row." Turns out, ducks love forming rows.

Living unnaturally in New York as I was, I hadn't the first clue about natural duck behavior. I assumed they were under supernatural influence because of me. I thought I was reading a sign in Nature that had some synchronistic meaning for me. It may sound weird that this would be my first guess, but as I said, I have lived a life of stranger things happening. Those stranger things, however, tended to mean something and that should have been my first clue that this was just what ducks do. The ducks who turned before me in the pond gave no well-timed meaning I could decipher except, just incidentally, to call out my self-involved paranoia. And, yeah, they probably wanted me off their rock.

After witnessing our ducks pull off this same move years later in Hawaii, I did something nigh unheard of in paranormal podcasting: I admitted I was wrong. I told on myself during our next show. I corrected the record for the public.

I was happy to solve the mystery because if everything is magical then nothing is magical. If everything is a sign then nothing is a sign. If all duck broods are turning to face me one at a time with meaning just for me then the gesture is meaningless.

If I cannot fess up when I discover that I'm wrong, at least to myself, then I'm living in fantasyland. I'm delusional. And I'm doing it to myself.

Chapter 1
Tiny Little Meepers

Tiny little meepers. That's what Carol and I called our new duckling family. One week old when we first met them, they were nameless and genderless to us. We bought them off of a homesteader Carol found on Facebook, a woman who raised multiple ponds worth of ducks. She brought them to us at a meetup in the parking lot of Miranda's Country Store in Keaau. It must have looked like the cutest drug deal in Hawaii's history. We fell in love with them before we even transferred them to our car.

For all that we had studied on ducklings before we became duck parents we were not prepared for how quickly they grew. Day one we introduced them to their temporary new home: a black plastic bin in our bathtub. They were only three days older than that when we let them run around a human child's playpen in the yard. And a few days later, they were living in a large encaged area plopped down on the front lawn. I built it for them with zero notice out of galvanized hardware cloth, UV light-resistant PVC piping, and camouflaged tarp. It was like having a batting cage on our front lawn full of pooping ducks.

The ducks didn't just physically grow exponentially. In three week's time, they had taught themselves the lay of the land. As soon as they were big enough to where we felt comfortable letting them wander, they were off to the races surveying everything.

We lived on the largest parcel in a four-home condo association. The ducks carved out a large swathe on our seventeen-and-a-half acres to run around in, mindful of the fence line and never heading up toward our neighbors at the top. I'm sure all of our neighbors' barking dogs played a role in forming their boundaries.

The ducks knew right out of the egg to stay away from dogs, cats, predatory birds, mongoose, rats, pigs, helicopters, airplanes, cars, trucks, and human guests. They learned our daily routine fairly immediately, too. We let them out at 9:00 a.m. every day. When we were late they told us all about it. They knew and know what to eat and what not to eat. They know to come back home and quack at us to give them snacks at 1:00 p.m.. Sometimes we acquiesce; sometimes we don't. When we don't, they don't press the issue for too long. They know how to read the room, so to speak. But when they come a quackin' to feed them dinner and tuck them away for the night at 4:30 p.m., we had better listen.

They knew and know all of this without parents or authorities. With only each other and the land, the air, the trees, other birds, their ancient inner compass, our morning and nightly routine, and whatever I don't know about ducks that I am missing, which I assure you is a lot. We thought we were giving them a schedule, but the truth is they knew how to schedule and live their lives.

They were training us.

***

When we finally named the eight tiny little meepers we were super inventive with it.

We named Blondie *Blondie* on account of her blonde feathering.

Black & White is a black duck with a white tuft on her head. My mom wanted us to name her *Zorro*, but it never stuck.

Then there is Welsh Harlequin, blessedly the only male, whose breed is already a cool name. No need for improvement there.

Chocolate we named *Chocolate* because she looked like chocolate.

Caramel & White practically named herself given her caramel complexion with a white tuft on her neck.

Penelope, a brown duck almost the complexion of Chocolate, was the only one to receive a human name. Carol named her *Penelope* because she looked like a Penelope.

Imua earned her Hawaiian name because we were stumped as to what to call her. Her feathering was primarily black interspersed with green-blue iridescence. Even at a young age she struck us as matriarchal and kindly. A friend said we should name her Imua, which is a Hawaiian word that means *keep going* and invokes leadership and strength. That is her.

Finally, there is Cohort, so named because when it came to picking on the other ducks she liked to conspire with Welsh Harlequin. She outgrew being his partner in crime after about a year, but the name stuck.

With time some of the ducks' feather colors changed, but not their names. Where others see tall, plump ducks, we still see our tiny little meepers. We still see Chocolate even though her dark brown feathering grows whiter with age. And we see Cohort even though she is independent and has mellowed out. Blondie's still a hot blonde. Welsh Harlequin sees her. Oh, yes he does.

***

Speaking of what others see, when it comes to these ducks, what people see is largely based on what they don't want to see. What they don't want to see is the ducks' equality. Likely this is because all of our evil human friends and family want to toss them with a salad and not feel like cannibals.

Ducks are no less than tiny people. Tiny people lacking arms, hands, and teeth. Tiny people with rounded bills and feet like clown shoes. Yes, they can fly. But they don't fly except to show off for us, because they know we like it. Yes, they can swim laps and fish like pros in water. But all we have for them are two blue kiddie pools from Ace Hardware. Mainly they wobble around and run at top speed. Top speed over rough terrain consisting of razor grass, dirt, and sharp lava rock.

Imagine yourself in a duck's body. How terrified would you be every moment of the day?

Big, scary world. No defenses at all. Clown feet. You'd contemplate eating a bullet at every sunset.

There is an entire video game subgenre where the goal is to investigate a frightening location, solve a mystery, and find your way out before getting caught by living killers who want to murder you in cold blood, or by hungry ghosts. In defense of your life, all you are allowed to do is sneak around with your flashlight, run, and hide. You can't fight back. This subgenre is not called *Love & Light* or *Find Joy*. It's called *Survival Horror*. That's what we imagine our lives would be in such a helpless state, and yet ducks, who are real-world examples of this, live in joy and inquisitiveness. They are happy little detectives. They certainly feel fear—quite often—but it's as a reflexive survival response. They very quickly snap back to their baseline as beings of joy and vast intelligence. Tiny little meepers are not dumb ducks. They are not meat. Born into what we would consider a hopeless predicament if we imagined it for ourselves, they are not merely survivors but thrivers. They only cower when they need to, not in constant anticipation of the next scary situation. Not living in a horrible memory, reacting to that, and calling that reaction *action*. Calling it *free will*. Calling it *living*.

Tiny little meepers are not human, so let's not *fowlopomorphize* ourselves any longer except to note that when they grew into older, bolder, brilliant child explorers, they earned a new nickname: *The Goonies*.

Because the movie.

Chapter 2
Blondie

If I remember correctly, Carol was the first to see it in Blondie when she was a tiny little meeper: the look in her eye revealed an intelligent person flapping around in there. And it's true: to look her in the eye is to notice that she radiates intelligence. She's constantly figuring things out. Figuring us out.

All of the ducks are little sleuths with one eye to the ground and the other to the sky. They are extremely curious, cocking their narrow heads when they're confused like any other narrow-headed person. But Blondie is always first to get it, whatever it is.

She was first to sidle up to us out in the yard. First to accept tasty dried grubs from our hands at snack time. First to fight the terror of my yellow raincoat, red shirts, and loud Bernie Sanders presidential campaign T-shirt with crisp white lettering over blue. She recognized the human dad beneath whatever horror those colors represented to her kind. In short, Blondie was first to trust us and to communicate that trust to us and therefore to her siblings. Unsurprisingly, she was first to fly.

We aren't the only ones to notice Blondie's intelligence. The other ducks have a certain deference towards her. And while there is no real pecking order, she is Welsh Harlequin's favorite sister-wife. If she straggles behind, he will wait for her. If she gets separated from the group, he will search low and lower for her. If everyone else wants to waddle off somewhere and she needs more bath time, he will stand by her side at the pool and the group will just have to wait before waddling anywhere, no matter who honks loudly in protest. Her even-colored blonde, practically white, feathering may have something to do with his attraction. He seems partial to blondes. But she's no stereotype, no party animal having more fun, no easy get. Clearly, she's no dumb blonde, either, and that horny honker loves every soft inch of her.

If the ducks needed a leader Blondie would make a sensible candidate. But they are more of a democratic people than that. To these ducks, higher intelligence doesn't translate into higher order.

Blondie is like the duck equivalent of a person who has had psychic awakenings: her advanced traits are noteworthy, but they don't elevate her to a higher echelon in duck society. She's not the guru of her duck clan. She's not their moral superior. She is their equal. They all have different traits that make them their own duck, but they don't dole out responsibilities based on their gifts or talents like Smurfs.

The flock recognizes that Blondie's intelligence is special, and their recognition is enough. It's enough because they cannot afford to have anyone stand out to predators, granted, but also because they each have at least one unique quality that makes them special. No one's uniqueness rates high or low.

No one's except for Penelope's, that is. Low.

Penelope has a handicap that leaves her unable to procreate and is a hazard in their eyes. A hazard they are willing to live with. Begrudgingly, for Welsh Harlequin. But that's just his loins talking. Everyone else is fine with her.

Can you imagine living in a world—living in your own psyche, really—where you don't have to lie about not wanting to feel special? A psyche where you just are that to everyone, and everyone to you, and it's no big deal?

A world where all humans are living authentic lives and so no one is trying to claw ahead, become a false leader, feel powerful and in control by reading from *The Book of Authenticity* and acting the part?

A psyche and a world where we're equals with ducks?

***

Often times the search for spiritual wisdom turns into a search for special powers. Finding words of wisdom that click with us and help us in small ways isn't enough for many of us. We lust after an ancient secret that will make us super heroes with psychic abilities, maybe give us a dash of omnipotence, and a golden path to a hero's future laid out before us by higher intelligence. Barring that, we'd settle for bragging rights over some spontaneous jerking while we fall asleep meditating.

If this describes you, how would you explain your insatiable thirst for feeling special to a duck like Blondie?

Do you know why you behave the way you do or is this too uncomfortable a subject to even think about?

Decent human parents make their children feel special, as they should. Making children feel special helps shape their self-worth. However, there comes a problem within adults who never grow out of that need and turn it into neediness. Turn it into a self-centered life. A life where they want to stand out. A life where they talk about oneness as code for how one of a kind they are. It doesn't have to be a life of full-blown narcissism but it's on that spectrum.

I envision Blondie cocking her head as those of you who are like this explain your specialness to her one by one. I imagine her pecking at the ground while you talk. It's not that she doesn't get you, it's that she's disinterested. She has better things to do than listen to you explain your uniqueness. Better things like eat spiders and live. Maybe, too, she understands something you hide from yourself: your life of trying to stand out is a life of unconsciously emulating unknowable oneness in the shallowest way you can conjure because you're insecure. I can't say for sure she knows this, but she is the smart one here.

I'll explain. Nothing makes you or any of us feel more insecure than the unknowable. You defend against it, those of you who do, by pretending that there is no such thing. One way you do this is by constructing a false sense of security and control in the known. You may feel secure in your knowledge. Secure in yourself. Secure in what tomorrow will bring. Secure that whatever happens is meant to be. But what happens when that facade of the known and the knowable falls away? The unknowable becomes the case. Since that facade is literally you, the unknowable is also literally you waiting to happen.

Why is that scary? Well, unlike unknowns, which can be answered given enough time, the unknowable cannot be answered at all. The unknowable is, therefore, not of time, which means you are not of time. Here's where human reality gets really insane: the you whom you pretend to be is emulating physical time by living a life of psychological time. You're a thought construct who is building a road to your future paved with the past. Nothing timeless, nothing unknowable may penetrate you without becoming you. Such short-lived experiences carry on in your memory, which you may choose to lay down more road with or leave behind as you travel.

See, the unknowable is not merely timeless like a classic song or a great work of art, it is timelessness. For one's self identity to be unknowable is to have died to the known. Since you are the known, are the past, modifying itself as it slings itself forward, this means you have to go. Not evolve. Not learn. *Not exist.*

Would that be so bad? I mean the body is already comprised of the past, it's already moving through time. Does it really need a self-awareness emulating that to carry out a bunch of harmful, made-up plots in life?

You know what you're like? You're like a person who has taken the lead role in a Broadway play and you don't even know what acting is.

I know, I know, you don't want to be that shell of a person, you want to be a soul. But currently you are braincells slapping together a self-image all the way through the body's lifespan. You call this thought construct the thinker or the doer or the feeler or the ego or just plain I. But this *I* is the brain emulating timelessness through a virtual reality construct. This *I* believes it is the one who is alive. This *I* is afraid of dying. Afraid, really, of not existing anymore. And this *I* does a clever thing: it covers up its fear by telling itself a story. A story about itself. A story it remembers from childhood.

I am unique.

I am special.

I am one of a kind.

How many billions of you believe this about you?

All of the billions, for even those of you who had terrible parents who read them a sad and deflating children's story, if they read to them at all, those who were neglected, those with low self-esteem, those who are now depressed, now angry at the world, those who feel completely useless, those who are suicidal—even you feel special in your loneliness. You don't frame it this way, but you feel special and unique and one of a kind in how awful you feel.

In the *Book of Us*, "Nobody Understands Me" and "Nobody Loves Me" are chapters that mirror "Everybody Gets Me" and "Everybody Loves Me." The delusions are as superficially different as the characters portraying them.

Aaaaah, the *Book of Us*. What a read.

Delusional. We're all delusional. And we're all in this together. That's its own special unity, isn't it?

However, when you see us honestly and thoroughly, the delusions clear up. It's not that you clear them up, they clear up despite you, hence why I speak about this in the annoying passive voice. Clarity strikes you down like a lightning bolt and with you goes your sense of others being other. You and I are no longer separate beings trapped together in delusion. You understand that there is only one consciousness being multiples of consciousnesses, therefore you are both. I am both. All "others" are both, including ducks.

If only you would realize this simple truth not as some idealistic blather, some truism, but realize it thoroughly beyond the words and the good feelings. Realize it in the meat and bones of your body—*that* deeply. So deeply that the body stops projecting you. Your absence in that moment may just afford the first Secret of Silence an opportunity to come alive and whisper sweetly through the body as its self identity. In that moment, truth becomes capitalized, like, *Truth*. Like how we capitalize *I*, because now Truth is I.

Truth, the capitalized version, is not just a word we humans put whatever meaning we like onto, it is living. It is formless and timeless. It is singular, not plural. It is absolute. And it is not an it, that's just the English language speaking.

Truth is Ultimate Intelligence, is Love, is Silence, is One. However, living in time as we do, and being psychological time as we are, we break fundamental oneness into multiple aspects. I'll be using those capitalized words and more to indicate the different aspects of oneness as we perceive them to be throughout this book. I mean, definitionally, they are simultaneously the case, but to our minds there are differences.

Seeing oneness as if it were lying in broken pieces is an inevitable problem with us. No one is at fault. When we speak Truth, we draw it into time. It takes form through us as relative thoughts and therefore is no longer absolute, no longer one, no longer living. In thought, Truth breaks apart into truths and we choose to give those truths whatever amount of "life" appeals to us. We remake them in our image and try to reanimate them like sacred Frankenstein's monsters. The only way to speak Truth and not have this happen is to be Truth. If we all realized Truth, that moment away from our trying to be special would actually be special.

Rest assured I'll spell all of this out in a less general way later in the book. Over and over again until you're sick of reading it, most likely. For now, just see the fact that Truth is only living in our world when it is speaking into time as a person, not when it is retold later. Not when it is mummified as a set of ideas people who are thought constructs run with into the future.

Most of us assume that Truth speaking through-and-as a person is a stage of mind rarified people live on or a fantasy that cannot be real. We take for granted that the truths they espouse are scraps for the rest of us to create with, discard, build upon, or try to live up to. We want there to be a handful of oracles who speak Truth for our benefit through gift, skill, or because God zapped them to Earth just for us, but it is incumbent upon all of us to be Truth speaking lest it inevitably get bastardized and warped, the source of our spiritual confusions.

From there power dynamics form between distinct and ever-dividing peoples who only come together as one in any lasting way through various forms of authoritarianism. If Truth becoming truths is us forgetting that we are one then authoritarianism is a sick and harsh reminder of our oneness pushing through the dreaming mind of a delusional people. Even our great democratic societies don't hold onto the equality of ducks forever.

Sorry to be the bearer of great news that sounds bad, but we can no longer afford to lazily ignore this. Still, Truth is not something we all must choose to speak like brainwashed zealots. No, being timeless means Truth is choiceless. Choiceless awareness, to be exact, and it is speaking to us even when we block it from speaking as us.

For all of us, consciously or unconsciously, the reality of what *choiceless* means takes on a terrifying notion. It strikes at the heart of our main fears: lack of control and, ultimately, nonexistence. Speaking as choiceless awareness means we're not the awareness speaking. It means we're out of control—or worse, dead.

Is being dead to Truth really worse? Or is it, like, you know... great?

For noise to be Silence is for noise to be dead. It's one or the other and we the noise want to exist. We want to jibber-jabber about Silence. Those of us who meditate will go so far as to claim that we're quieting our chattering minds. But if you're the one quieting your mind and you're the noise that needs to be quieted, then you're still being noise. Is this not self-evident?

You are noise. The noise of the brain. Assuring yourself that you're something higher or more detached from the body than brain noise is just more noise. Is it possible for the brain to understand this absolutely clearly without running away? Without making it conceptual, a thought experiment, or a religious statement? Is it possible for the brain to see the fact of its own matter so transparently that it stops projecting noisy ol' you completely, full-stop?

Is it possible, in other words, for the self to die while the body remains alive? Not go into a coma or have the personality overhaul of brain damage. I'm asking if the brain can stop making noise completely. If it can, then is that silence capitalized? Is it Silence? Is it formless intelligence?

Silence has an intelligence of its own?

Silence has an intelligence of its own.

Remember that Truth and Silence are one. But from where we stand they look like two. It is from where we stand that we're asking if the Intelligence of Silence becomes the 1st-person intelligence of the body when the normal self sense has dissolved. Does such a one choicelessly speak Truth?

I don't know if this is making any sense to you yet, but I bet Blondie gets it. She gets everything. She could explain it better in a few short quacks.

Chapter 3
Welsh Harlequin

I do an amazing vocal impression of Welsh Harlequin's inner monologue. I said earlier that his being the only male was a blessing. That's because male ducks are super sexually charged and, well, just a wee bit rapey. Seven sister-wives is enough for one male—except he will not touch Penelope with his ten-inch (give or take nine) pole. So make that six sister-wives. I'll let you guess how my impression of him goes.

We didn't know he was male when he was a tiny little meeper because all of the ducklings made the same meeping noises. It was only much later in their lives— roughly one human week—when they began to develop their mighty quacks, honks, and assorted bike horn noises. All, that is, except Welsh Harlequin. Drakes, which is what humans call male ducks, make a quiet, almost croaking sound. It's like vocal fry without the vocals.

Library-quiet though he is, we can still hear Welsh Harlequin clearly through the window, down the field, even in the roaring wind. Even in downpours. Even in downpours through the roaring wind with the TV blasting so we can hear it over the storm. Nothing drowns out the mighty pterodactyl croak of a drake. It's not a volume issue so I'm guessing it's a frequency thing. Even when they're all huddled close together we can hear him. Hear him through the din of his sister-wives' loud bicycle horns. Whatever the reason is for this 8th natural wonder, his whispery ASMR croak will not be denied.

Another trait he developed that his sisters did not was a curly tail feather. I suppose it matches his corkscrew-shaped penis, which, thank Nature, I have never seen. I have, however, been privy to the horror show that is hot duck-on-duck action. It's hard not to feel terrible for the lady ducks because it always looks like he's overpowering them. Actually, it looks like he's riding a bike with his orange legs in motion while tugging on their necks. Tugging like an evil black knight yanking the reigns of his steed. Not that knights peddle horses, but you get my mixed metaphor.

Though my impression of his cruel inner monologue will never confess this, in reality, the ladies often bob their heads up and down at the pool asking him for sex or telling him they're ready. Almost as often, the ladies have sex with each other. Sometimes they do it to dominate each other; sometimes for fun. Sometimes they aren't in the mood for Welsh Harlequin and the ol' corkscrew. This doesn't stop him. He can't help himself. He's the Casanova of tiny feathered men.

With his emerald scalp plumage, Dijon mustard bill, thin necklace of white, 50-shades-of-gray backside, and safety-orange feet, this brown-barrel-chested duck is magnificent. And he knows it. Unfortunately for him, his gorgeous looks and confidence have not made him a leading man in any way. He's not even a beloved figure amongst his flock. Emasculating truth be told, he is tolerated, mostly. Perhaps this is why he hates Penelope. Her unshakeable self-esteem in the face of being slightly deformed is a backwards mirror reflection of this beautiful narcissist who secretly hates himself.

***

When you have no arms, no teeth, clown shoe feet, and a tendency not to fly, procreation is your best weapon against extinction. Welsh Harlequin got the memo. So did his sister-wives. The act itself is just gross to us humans because we make Nature gross. Gross and scary. Gross and scary and to be tamed or destroyed as we see fit.

How we see fit to dominate Nature is primarily through one of two ways. Either through a form of psychopathy where every other living being is treated like an object we choose to let live or destroy, depending on what we want from them, or through infantilization where we try to cuddle with all the nonhumans we deem worthy of our smothering love. Usually we do both at the same time.

When Welsh Harlequin smothers a lady duck it isn't for love, it's for sex. And that sex is not the assault we make it out to be. It looks like how our sexual predators hurt others with sex, but duck sex is for rapid procreation, for fun, and also for relaying information. I can't say all of what information, but certainly at least this: if a duck gets lost or otherwise separated from the flock, when she comes back, he will chase her around until he catches her and have sex with her on the spot. I don't think any of our female ducks like this at all.

Some duckologist somewhere will probably tell you he is asserting his dominance. I'm no duckologist so I'll go with what I see: I think he is trying to positively identify her. Obviously, he can see and hear her, but I think there must be another sense where he feels her from the inside to be certain it is her. Perhaps his corkscrew leaves an imprint and when the grooves line up, *Welcome back!*

Because, frankly, he is just not that dominant over them in any other situation.

In fact, Welsh Harlequin can be quite the gentleman. At dinner and snack time he lets the ladies eat and drink first. When it comes to taking charge, more often than not he isn't leading them around the yard or protecting them beyond being a lookout when it is his turn to monitor the land and sky for predators. They all take turns with those duties.

That said, I hear him now as I type these words, talking to the flock. He is a spectacular goofball—the chattiest of all the ducks. Also, the quietest. Also, the loudest. Welsh Harlequin is a living, breathing, sex machining paradox.

Sexual energy is in his occupational description, but it does not describe him as a duck. How that sexual energy manifests as an act is, as I said, multipurpose. However else we consider it to be manifesting— beautiful, disgusting, or not considering it at all—is us denying reality by either making up stories or ignoring the subject.

***

Much as I hate to admit it even I don't truly know Welsh Harlequin's inner voice. It's easy to get caught up in my cleverness and forget that I am making him up. Making him up in my mind's eye as an id-driven sex maniac. And contaminating my wife's idea of him with the force of my taboo humor, which reflects the gross sexual weapons in the human arsenal more than anything the duck is doing.

My ability to perform psychological alchemy for the sake of comedy gold is just fine in the context of Carol's and my relationship, but if I were to sell you on ducks being nothing more than conduits for sexual energy I would be doing everyone a major disservice. Especially Welsh Harlequin, the poor chap. And yet, when we hear about the human body containing a latent energy that rises up through chakra centers from the base of the spine to ultimately explode out the top of one's head, thrusting one into union with the cosmos, we often hear that it is a mysterious type of sexual energy.

I suppose that does sound sexual. But has it been described accurately or is it more like my impression of Welsh Harlequin?

We humans tend to confuse things so that we may label our confusion "complicated." It makes us feel above the simple. Above beings like Welsh Harlequin, who, while he may be a crude, sexy beast, at least he's not dumb enough to confuse his sex drive with an energy that rises up the spine and blows out his cranium into the universe at large. He's not even dumb enough to put that sentence together. He's busy pleasuring the ladies. (Minus Penelope.)

I think when it comes to spiritual pontification, we often get lost in our metaphors and start believing they are the real. That's the case here. Sexual energy can be likened to any movement of rising and exploding. A volcano going off. Opening a bottle of warm champagne. A psychotic man dressed as a clown blowing up hotdog-shaped balloons at children's parties until they burst. The kids cry. He giggles. Giggles the Clown, that's his name. Who invited Giggles and why?

Not important. The important thing is that orgasmic release is not the same movement as produced by the energy we're talking about, even if you throw the word "sacred" in there. This energy, the real energy, is a massive Secret of Silence—it is the Will of Silence.

Silence has a will of its own?

Silence has a will of its own.

You see, while the Intelligence of Silence choicelessly speaks Truth in the form of wise words through a person, or even as a person, it also performs physical actions by moving the body in spontaneous, coordinated ways. This mover and shaker is what we are calling, the *Will of Silence*. On occasion, the Will of Silence may utilize sexual energy, and that's how we know it is not sexual energy. Sexual energy is a means to an end.

For example, if you have an affliction with a body part —let's say your right knee—the Will of Silence, which behaves like a foreign willpower in the body, may maneuver your right hand to tap out a line over and over on your skin, going from the genitals to the knee. It may then masturbate you and at the point of orgasm slam your thighs shut so that you don't outwardly climax. You may then find your body convulsing a bit and your hips moving sharply left and right as that sexual energy travels internally to... guess where? That's right, the knee!

I'm no biologist so I won't pretend to know what the material process going on there is. Perhaps something to do with directing endorphins to the knee because they have a healing capability with certain injuries? I don't know. Just throwing that out there as a possibility. However it plays out scientifically, I don't need to know. It happens. It works. Your knee feels better as a result.

Now, let's talk about the initial act of that energy rising. It's true that it rises up from the base of the spine, which is... you know... *down there*. So why aren't we calling it sacred butt energy? Why isn't it more like a grand and satisfying fart winding its way up the spine? Not enough of a selling point? At least it's gender-neutral. Ah. But wait. We are also told that it is a recursive exploding force. It explodes as it rises. Over and over, I guess, because it rises and falls as many times as you activate it. This could certainly bring to mind a vision of both penis power and female orgasmic waves. It ends in a climax out the top of one's head, right? Totally horny words. Welsh Harlequin would approve. Small problem here: none of these details we have been taught about the Will of Silence are true. I know from 25 years of living with this.

What is true is that this energy rises the initial time and then it's there, forever fused with you. It doesn't need to keep rising and falling and you cannot make it rise and fall. Also, the notion that it explodes inside you before it rises is just crap. Crap that either stems from mixing up the metaphor for the real or from people experiencing some other explosive internal event that they are wrongly attributing to this mysterious force. The force rises and you feel it surging, but no explosion.

One of the accompanying myths about the Will of Silence being sexual energy is that you need to conserve it. Celibacy is not purity. A chaste mind has nothing to do with sex, it has only to do with being innocent, and that is the purity one needs. There are other reasons to conserve sexual energy, but not for the sake of purity. Welsh Harlequin will be happy to hear it.

Be simple. Be honest. Be curious about yourself. Do not be answered. You are not answered. You are not certain. Carving out a reality tunnel and justifying that limited existence of yours through rationalizations and gut feelings has nothing to do with the limitless energy you've been told sits idle like a foreign engine at the base of your spine until you master the proper techniques to jumpstart it. This seemingly other willpower, this miraculous natural force, is you. But only you when you, the echo chamber of a reality tunnel reading this right now, collapse under the weight of your own lie. Better that than under the weight of Welsh Harlequin.

Perhaps we should change the analogy. The Will of Silence is not sexual, it's celebration. When you, the psychological time construct being projected by the body, are no longer present, *timeless being* comes alive in the very same body. Perhaps all the psychic explosions are fireworks and party favors. It's a major celebration. Happy re-birthday!

But don't invite Giggles the Clown. He only paints himself to look like he's down to clown. His white van with blacked out windows screams something else entirely. And muffles the screams of children.

Something tells me Welsh Harlequin might appreciate Giggles's approach to socialization.

Carol and I love him anyway.

Chapter 4
Imua

If she had hips like ours she'd have mom hips. Pretty much from birth, mom hips and a maternal sensibility to go with them. She's built rock solid in body and psyche, that Imua. The ducks may not have a leader but they certainly respect her like one. Nobody messes with her, not even hyper-sexual Welsh Harlequin. She has her way with him on her terms.

Imua is such a kind-hearted and giving duck, she no doubt is the glue of her tribe. Even on those pantingly hot summer days when the ducks don't feel like they can do anything but sleep in the shade and eat, cut off from their usual ability to run free—those days when they get nippy with each other—I don't think I've ever seen Imua lose her temper with any of her kin.

Imua is the sort of duck who waits for you when you're feeling slow and running last. She's the duck who is there for you, right by your side when you need her most. Or pulling up the rear if that's what's needed.

Once, when I was cleaning their run, from the corner of my eye I caught a gigantic blood-red centipede running full-speed on all legs toward me. Imua saw it, too, and immediately sprang into action. She ran up behind it, bit at it like a vintage typewriter madly churning out an espionage thriller, scooped it up in her bill, and shook it side to side like a vicious dog murdering a... well... anything, really. Then she tossed it in the air away from me, ran over to it, and repeated the process. When that snake-like critter was good and dead, she gulped down her hard won snack in one long, tasty, fiery bite.

Imua is not just her brood's protector, she is mine. I am forever indebted.

***

Imua is intelligent. She's stable. She's nurturing. She's fierce. She's creative. And I swear she was born knowing exactly who she is. That type of self-knowing, which leaves no room for insecurity, is an energy all its own.

She's like the mother archetype come to life in a duck, you know? She is a goddess too humble to assume such a title. Nevertheless, I know goddess energy when I see it and she is Imua.

But that energy isn't really a goddess, is it? *Goddess energy* is a metaphor, a description of her maternal strengths, especially her impulse to protect, which are what she leads with in life. Imua does indeed fit the human archetypes of mother and goddess, but what is an archetype if not a primordial pattern of behavior that humans notice and whip up stories about? Stories that develop a life of their own. Stories that, once originally told by people, perpetually tell themselves through other people, like an artificial intelligence that actually is conscious.

It's fashionable these days for human men and women to talk about goddess energy like it's a real energy. To the extent that they are talking about an archetype, I suppose it could be. As an explanation for the mysterious, unknowable force that awakens and moves a person as if another will has come alive within the body? Not so much.

Goddess energy. We like to use grandiose terms, humans do. Westernized ones, anyway. I don't know about others. Westernized human people have this grab-bag of performative Scrabble words they toss on the board to win spiritual recognition.

Goddess energy. No one ever talks about god energy, they just talk about God. God as a paternal entity who we must fear and placate. Goddess energy is more benign and is something we may tap into. It can take on a persona, or be given one. It's far more airy than solid. In many ways goddess energy is the antithesis of God.

I rarely hear goddess energy enthusiasts mention God. They're too busy rebelling against God to talk about him—and for good reason given all the atrocities we've done in the name of that losing three-letter Scrabble word. But religious rebellion is moving the goal post. Babbling about God and goddess energy are fundamentally the same game of externalizing and gendering unknowable Being.

That may sound rich coming from me given that on numerous occasions I have written about hearing a nameless, disembodied, female voice whom I've called, simply, *Her*. I've heard Her throughout my life in various contexts ranging from dreams that were interrupted by Her to impart a message, to a so-called *alien abduction* where we held a brief conversation. I once had the I AM universal consciousness experience, which we'll get to later in the book. Guess who showed up at the end with a cheesy message for humanity? That's right, Her. All of this is why one of the dedications in my book *Urgency.* (yes, punctuated with a period) is to Her.

Is she a goddess? Is she an aspect of me? Am I an aspect of her? Is there a difference in any of this?

Given that a thus-far formless female voice has made herself apparent in my life from time to time, and given that I now have an impersonal willpower living alongside me in the body, how do I know she isn't the much-ballyhooed goddess energy pouring life into me?

For starters, I've also been talked to by ethereal male voices over the years. I don't feel as much connection with them, which is why I haven't dedicated any books to *Him*. Her voice is singular whereas I can think of at least three instances in which I heard or conversed with distinct male voices. So that's a factor.

Also, there is something more... well... urgent about Her voice than any of the males imparting their wisdom. She sounds stern and empathetic at the same time. Formal. Like a good teacher. Almost British, but not quite. If she has a favorite musical it's *The Sound of Music*, put it that way. She's got a Julie Andrews compassionate strength vibe to her. In almost every instance it's as if she is desperate for us (or maybe just me, but I think all of us) to wake up to our full human expression. Her desperation is tempered with understanding precisely why we do not.

Hers is the voice of existential urgency. Hers is the voice that compels as it nurtures. Hers is the voice of Imua. This does not mean she is a feminine archetype come alive through Imua or me, but it does mean she knows how to play the role. Since she has, in fact, spoken to me, and since the Intelligence of Silence, which moves the body with a knowledge base that is not my own, is living within this body, I know that they are not one and the same. And I know that neither is goddess energy.

Incidentally, I also know that whatever other energies Imua is, she is her own energy fueled by centipedes and love. She makes that clear everyday.

Chapter 5
Chocolate

The first duck to fly was Blondie, showing off her intelligence. For her it was just a little hop up in place and a flutter. Her siblings quickly followed suit, some better than others. Still to this day, some better than others.

Penelope, for instance, still isn't really going anywhere. And Black and White, she can just sort of hop up and fly about a foot or two horizontally from where she stands. But the rest, they can full on fly if they want.

In the morning, when I go down to the duck run to let them out for breakfast, I see it's Cohort and Caramel & White who do the long distance flying. They'll back themselves up and fly across the run right when I open the gate.

Welsh Harlequin, he jumps up and helicopters in place, then flies out. He's always got to be the most majestic flyer.

These days, Black & White usually starts off the flying in the morning. Just with her little hop because I think she likes my reaction, which is the joyful surprise one emotes to a child who does something they think is impressive. It's difficult being joyful on my own early in the morning, but ducks have an antidote for that.

Now a duck expert, or "duckspert," as such a one might rightly prefer to be called, may tell you that the ducks believe making me laugh and hoot and holler is what they have to do to get me to let them out in the morning. They want out of their prison and they want breakfast. They want their pools of fresh water. They want to run around and eat new bugs from different places.

Well, duckspert be damned. The fact is, I let them out and put them back whether they perform or not. Either way they get fed, they forage, and they have their needs met by me. And it always was this way, long before they chose to show off for my amusement. It certainly doesn't get me to move faster. I have to untie the gate and open it up to let them out. In fact, watching them slows down the process of releasing them.

No, they simply love making me laugh because it brings me joy, and they *are* joy. Small embodiments of joy. They love forging a connection between our species through our shared language of mirthful laughter.

Of all the ducks, Chocolate—who at this point should maybe be called *White Chocolate* because her head and neck continue to slowly bleach white (she looks more like a powdered donut than a pure chocolate)—has taken to flying back from the house to the duck run when I walk them home before sunset. One random evening, she decided to blow past us as we slowpokes waddled down the hill. She loved my pleasantly surprised reaction and turned it into a nightly ritual that goes like this:

I fill their water containers in the run and then walk up to the house to get their food dish. They follow me, single-file, nodding their approval and egging me on with their quacks. On the way back down the hill to their run, Chocolate waits for me to say, "Chocolate! Chocolate, fly! Fly, Chocolate! Fly!" I usually speak these magic words while flapping my free left arm and holding their dish of fermented seed and greens in my right hand. That's when she takes off, leaving us in her wake.

Chocolate gets the assignment. There's no training involved, only communication. Only wanting to hear my reaction so she can respond. She looks at me and then she flaps away because she knows I like it. She enjoys throwing me into a giggle fit as much as I enjoy laughing.

I don't know if ducks have giggle fits or not. If they do, they're not obvious. But ducks certainly understand laughter's origin in the heart. It is a sign of a blissful connection with Chocolate, not the torturous antics of one Giggles the Clown or his sidekick, the Holy Spirit. Weird combo, right? I agree. But have you ever heard of holy laughter?

There was a time when videos of charismatic evangelical congregations falling off their chairs in hysterical fits of laughter were all the rage on social media. The charismatics call it *holy laughter*. Some competing fundamentalist religious types chalk it up to devil energy imported from India tricking them into acting the buffoon. That's what they believe the Will of Silence is: a trick of the devil begotten from Hindu mediation and yoga. Foreign devilry at its silliest.

Natural laughter does not well up by accident. Nor by magic. Nor by craze. It's not the same as the type of internal welling of uncontrollable, gut-busting, drop-to-the-floor-and-convulse-like-a-fish-out-of-water laughter often erroneously attributed to the Will of Silence. But it does have its place as we shall see.

***

When Carol and I were raising ducks in the brief few weeks that they were ducklings, we trained them to love and trust us, but not too much. Not too much because we didn't want them to feel as though they had to run up to us for hugs or let us constantly dote on them. We didn't want them begging us to let them inside the house or feel a sense of loss when we left them. Who needs needy ducks?

Also, we didn't want them feeling totally comfortable around humans. If they ever got lost, we didn't want them talking to strangers who might look at them and see, not children, but, dinner. (Talking to you, Giggles. Not so much you, Holy Spirit.)

To this day, Chocolate refuses to eat out of my hand at snack time. Our special connection is purely her flying before supper. The joy of flight is our bond. It's not a harm. It's not a torture. It's not an unspoken collaboration between two beings with compatible psychological dysfunctions. It never grows stale. It's a loving expression of real relationship. It's doing for someone else and you both feel the same great feeling. You're in it together. It's two beings living laughter in one timeless moment.

I think if Chocolate didn't do anything to warrant my glee—if I just laughed and cheered for no reason—she would be confused. Anyone would be confused. Hell, I would be confused. Laughter serves a purpose whether you are conscious of it or not. When it comes to energies we call *spiritual*, that purpose gets obscured by guesswork and desire. When we act out these wrong guesses, and if we really commit, we look bizarre to normal people.

Wrong guess number one is that laughing fits are a sign of the awakened Will of Silence. It's not just charismatics who participate in the myth-making; some nonreligious individuals claim they have had laughing fits so uncontrollable that they must be a sign they've activated the mysterious ascending force. However, most of the material I've found on social media pertaining to this is a debate around whether certain charismatic church leaders are invoking the force in their flock, so let's dial in on that first.

Why do made-for-public-access-TV evangelical churches encourage their flock to fall off their pews and writhe on the floor, enraptured in uncontrollable laughing spells? They might tell you it's not due to any encouragement on their part; rather, it's a literal showing of God's power that causes this. And again, other fundamentalist Christians outside of their sect believe it is a trick of the devil taking the form of what so many Hindus lovingly refer to as *serpent energy*. To these Christians, *serpent* equals *devil*.

Oh, man. Satan hath invaded the megachurch through demon-possessed ministers and old people writhing around like "Curly" from *The Three Stooges*. It doesn't get more hilarious than that. Sorry to say, fundamentalists, but the uncontrollable laughter scripts itself.

Let me offer a third position in the debate: the insane laughing spells are neither the work of Jesus nor of the serpent, but of regular people who spend their days wearing puckered scowls across their faces, who need to act out their taboos. I'm no psychologist, but does it take one to see what's at work here? Puckered face energy, not ascending puckered butt energy. Broken people taking their cues from, and mimicking, their drunk-looking preacher who, with the aid of some plants in the audience, is showing them what to do and giving them permission to do it.

Of course this doesn't answer the problem of nonreligious individuals succumbing to such laughter on their own, just the megachurches acting intoxicated. What of these people, then? Are their uncontrollable hysterics caused by a rising serpent doing butt play?

I don't know. Maybe it's Jesus this time. Or Satan. Or they're overly tired. Maybe they're high. I just know it isn't Mystery with a capital "M" energy. Not, in other words, the Will of Silence.

Whatever the cause, it's a small "m" mystery. Probably the telephone game. You know the one, where you heard someone claim that someone else said spontaneous laughter was a symptom of this energy being alive in them and so now you're showing symptoms, too? That game. The one where you're unconsciously remedying your feelings of inadequacy and meaninglessness with the medicine of feeling special.

This whole laughter business is an example of our copying the awakened state so that we never have to wake up. We can just incorporate aspects of it bit by bit into our dream and stay asleep. It keeps the nightmare of waking up at bay.

Why would we treat waking as a nightmare, you ask?

We are a backwards people. Right now we believe we are awake, and that belief is the sleep. Only the cessation of the dreamer is the waking up. The furtherance of the dreamer is a long nap. We understand this when someone like me says it out loud but then go right back to conniving ways of attaining capabilities and aspects of the awakened state to power up our siesta. We all do this, not just the blatant posers.

Bluntly stated, we want to be more powerful in life, not dead. Death sounds more like sleep than waking up, and again, this is because we're backwards. Scoff if you will, but the fact remains that while you wear your phony spiritual awakening giddiness like a badge of ascension, laughter has a real power only needed by the awakened, not by the sleeper "ascending." Its purpose is not a mystery to such. And its purpose cannot be emulated by you without you looking like a donkey. A donkey with a million likes and subscribers, naturally, but a donkey nonetheless.

The true power of laughter is yet another Secret of Silence. I'm going to whisper it to you whether you're ready to hear it or not. You're not, but here goes....

For fully actualized humans living on the other side of sleep, laughter acts as a buffer between absolute perfection, which is Love felt as impersonal joy, and all of the hurt one also feels on life's behalf. This includes one's own life. Laughter to such a one is not random, not pointless, not sadistic, not a personal defense mechanism, not about being good-humored or bad. Not even about relating to ducks like Chocolate. Like same-sided magnets, laughter is the necessary bouncing force that repels the singular, impersonal, "emotional" quality of absolute self-awareness from the plethora of pains and confusions experienced by personal self-awareness. All of that verbiage can be contained in a single word: *compassion*.

Tears of compassion release into laughter and that mediates the absolute and the relative.

The reason I am explaining this to you and not to Chocolate isn't because you have a better chance of understanding it than she, but because she doesn't need to hear it. She's a fully actualized duck. She knows laughter as our special bond. That's good enough for her. Good enough for both of us, to be completely honest.

What you need to know about you is that the words we use in a spiritual context, like *enlightened* and *awakened*, should only mean *wholly conscious*. The difference between someone bumbling through life and someone who is enlightened is only the difference between someone who doesn't consciously live real human nature and someone who does. We are all that real human nature whether we are conscious of it or not. Isn't it time we live our whole nature consciously?

When we don't, those of us who care about the subject at all scramble for that next sign or symptom of our growing enlightenment. The symptoms we discover are lies that are compelling precisely because they draw from the actual. The actual of which we are unconscious. We make it conscious in a delusional way that fits our lifestyle, not a way that enlightens us.

That's why the real outsider with no interest in this may find uproarious laughter to be a bizarre indicator of having tapped into higher spiritual energy or having been tapped by the Holy Spirit. Those are delusions, yes. The laughter they promote has psychological origins, yes. But the reason the religious leaders chose laughter wasn't random or crazy, even if it was unconscious. Laughter serves a real purpose for the awakened, yet these leaders cannot understand what it is because they're asleep.

So what do they do?

They bend compassionate humor to the nonsensical physics of their dream. And then they encourage you to dream with them.

They don't want to know the truth. Neither do you.

Even though they do. Even though you do, too.

Chapter 6
Black & White

Black & White is our most colorful duck. Even as a babe she had a little lumpy pompadour-like stitch of white feathering atop her otherwise black head, which is why my mother wanted to name her *Zorro*. But Carol and I? We stuck with *Black & White*. We weren't sure why at the time. Maybe it had to do with the irony of her being such a colorful character who set herself apart without rebelling from her family. She just had this aloneness to her right out of the egg, even though she stuck by them.

At the very least ducks are a tightly-knit group for safety reasons. They tend to waddle in single file to look bigger than they are and to survey all of their environment. Black & White, however, has no problem trailing far behind. She has no problem being by herself. She is singular in that way amongst the ducks.

Black & White is in duck society but not of duck society. Because of this I think she understands her family in a way that they cannot reciprocate. This fact never made her judgmental, and it didn't prompt them to reject her. She is not an outcast. Contrary, she is loved and respected. She is treated well and treats everyone well. She hangs out with Penelope when Penelope lags behind. By all appearances they are best friends.

What makes Black & White so colorful is that she has her own sense of time and a strong sense of herself. Sometimes she gets sick of running around and plops down in the cushy grass for a snooze wherever she is. Just as often we will find her lost in a daydream while enjoying a carefree bath, only to snap out of it and wonder where her flock ran off to. In those moments she will call out to them and if she hears no response, go looking for them.

Black & White truly is an individual. Every human person I know believes they're an individual too because they've got a name, a point of view, a personality. The majority of them see otherness out through two holes in their face and think, 'I am me.' Really, what they are is an embodied manifestation of the stream of human consciousness. If that self sense were to dissolve—if such a one were to step out of the stream, as it were—perhaps that one would know what individuality actually is. And maybe Black & White has done her version of this: stepped out the stream of duck consciousness.

If she were human she might have a holiday named after her. Might be worshipped. Or feared and bullied. Maybe killed for the blasphemy of her existence. Truth is, that type of hierarchical thinking has no place in freedom and these ducks are free. Free to be every shade of duck. Free to be as they are, not as we define them, which usually results in shoving them in not just metaphorical but literal cages.

Black & White can certainly hang with her group and be in the group, and she is most of the time. But like I said, she may just as easily decide to step away and revel in aloneness. This is part of who you are when you're authentically an individual. Not as a rebellion. Not to be antisocial. Not to be narcissistic. Not because you want to feel special and unique. Not as a reaction to fear.

Anti-intuitive though it may be, a human individual is not one whose mind is set solid as a rock against the current of human consciousness. Most of us have been taught differently. Taught the opposite, in fact. Most of us believe we need to strengthen ourselves, better ourselves, or add onto ourselves with knowledge, experiences, and abilities to stand apart from the crowd. We think we need to learn how to stand firmly in, against, or swim with, the current of society to be the best *me* we can be.

Truth may be understood as the conscious ocean that contains all streams. Truth is a different story than the ones we tell. Truth says an individual is one who has individuated from the human consciousness stream, not within it. One whose brain-body complex has dissolved the self completely for Truth to become the voice and the action of the body. Truth says, "You may hear my words and make wisdom of them and carry on in the human stream in strife and sorrow. Or the brain projecting you may see the futility of you and turn you off. I become you in that moment. I become the self-awareness of the body, not just fleeting moments of universally applicable statements about living rightly that you try and fail to live by."

That's not a direct quote. Truth is less wordy.

For humans, Truth living as one's self-awareness is an all or nothing proposition because Truth is whole. Truth is individual. Is it the same for ducks?

Does Black & White identify as a duck in form and history only? Is that why she is so relaxed? Is this how she is able to live in duck society while no longer being of duck society?

To lack the fear of not fitting in because you see so clearly—you see what society is and you see what the individual is—I wonder if this how Black & White sees. Is her inner world clear like this? Is everything black and white to Black & White?

Is that the root of her colorful nature?

Chapter 7
Penelope

Besides Welsh Harlequin there is only one other duck bestowed the gift of a lifelong vocal impression by yours truly. That lucky duck is Penelope. Unlike Welsh Harlequin, I'm pretty sure I nailed her thoughts for real. She's a duck who wears her heart on her feathery sleeve.

Muddy brown plumage with white undertones and a misshapen body, Penelope is *The Ugly Duckling*, if in the end of that story the swan didn't have to realize her own beauty while figuring out she wasn't a duck at all. Penelope wouldn't need to. She has healthy self-esteem and loves herself regardless of what other ducks think. Plus she's an actual duck. That helps.

As less a result of her awkward appearance and more because of her disabilities she is the outcast, the forsaken, and yet she knows her worth and just wants to be accepted as the beautiful duck that she is.

Penelope, more than most human people I have met, is self-actualized. Not in the same way Black & White is. It's more like Penelope knows that who she is isn't the sum of her parts—those parts being her fat, bendy, sink-pipe neck, which practically drags on the ground, and her crooked butt. What I don't think she knows—what I hope she has forgiven and forgotten—is that her problems are my fault. At least the butt part.

When we first introduced the ducklings to their bigger duck cage we had a doghouse in there for them to hide in. One morning at dawn something spooked them. They meeped away until we came out to find them all crammed behind the doghouse. They were bottlenecked between the cage and the house and so I had to move the doghouse to free them. I moved it unevenly, though, only dragging one side out. The other side pushed further in toward the steel mesh resulting in poor Penelope's backside accidentally getting crushed. She recovered but her hiney was never the same.

Penelope remains crooked in the back, which makes her prone to tipping over whenever she walks on uneven ground, scratches her head with her gnarled, escargot-looking feet, or tries to stand up proud and tall to flap water off her wings. Her crooked butt makes it a chore, and sometimes an impossible one, to step into either of the kiddie pools if at least one of them isn't sloping downward to lower the point of entry. It also leaves her unable to receive the sweet, rapey lovin' from Welsh Harlequin or lay eggs. In total, her deformity makes her a liability to her flock.

Rather, *I* made her a liability to her flock. If she knew I was responsible, she never let on. Perhaps she forgave me right away. More importantly, she never let her handicap drag down her self-worth.

Penelope isn't depressed about it. Never was. She has always been resilient. She refuses to act the part of a liability no matter how her flock shuns her at times. At all times by Welsh Harlequin, but on rare occasions by her sisters, too.

Her sisters still accept her most days. On those hot, sunny afternoons that leave them irritable, a couple of them may nip at her. Even so, she always has allies. Black & White is a great friend to her, as are Chocolate and Imua. Mainly all the girls love her and it is only Welsh

Harlequin who refuses to give her a passing glance except to chase her off, wings outstretched, mouth agape, at breakfast and dinner. His hungry monster act probably looked a shade scarier back when birds were dinosaurs. After a billion years of evolution he looks like a toy airplane taking a nosedive.

Because I don't let Welsh Harlequin drive her off the food dish while I'm around, Penelope looks to me as her protector. Sometimes, she'll even taunt him and then run to me so that he won't dare retaliate. Such is her confidence. She grows fat and happy with her status at the bottom.

And she loves me. Of all the ducks, she is most affectionate, charging at me whenever she sees me. This is one way ducks show appreciation: head down like a linebacker, full steam ahead. But not to hit, just to run up to you like that and then mutter-honk joyfully.

Another way ducks acknowledge you is by darting their heads to the side quickly and repetitively like the clubber dudes in that ancient *Saturday Night Live!* sketch, "The Roxbury Guys." All the while they'll make a clicking sound like the Smoke Monster from *LOST*. Penelope is no stranger to doing that, either.

She was not the first to brave my extended hand at snack time, but once she dared my temptation she made it a habit to always run up and eat dried grubs from my palm. Even that's awkward, though, because she doesn't peck them into her mouth with any real skill. She tears at them like a Rottweiler with a bloody steak, often biting a finger or two by accident. Even so, once she realized I was safe, she let me pet her while feeding her. My reward, I suppose.

I definitely have a special bond with Penelope. Quite possibly Stockholm Syndrome. She loves me and I her.

Of all the ducks she is the only one with an archetypal story like this, an Everyduck journey similar to humans. Perhaps if we were to follow ducks around all day we'd see exactly what shapes and reshapes their personalities. We'd know that their life experiences run deeper than our current observations of them. Stunningly brilliant observations like, "Ha, ha! They waddle funny!" And, "Look at 'em snap at mosquitos!"

Yep, brilliance like that.

Regardless of Man's superior waterfowl discoveries, of all the ducks there is only one Penelope. And we do have a relationship different from her siblings, it's not just in my head. She has so much personality and confidence, it's impossible to ignore her individuality. A lesser duck would have grown despondent from not being able to lay eggs or know the lust of a drake. I'm not hanging around them most of the day to protect her from bullying or to feel guilty and cheer her on when she falls on her gullet. She's on her own. She is fine with that as long as she still belongs to her family. She just wants to be a duck. A big, beautiful duck.

***

Penelope's life is one heckuva story for us humans to digest. It's easy to relate to the ugly duckling part. Who among us hasn't suffered from poor self-esteem at some point? Or from being picked on?

And then the human version of the story usually develops into one of coping by maintaining a healthy outlook on life and learning to feel comfortable in your own skin. Or not coping until much later in life, if at all. These, roughly, are our paths forward.

Penelope never had to choose a path. Penelope never had to therapy her way into realizing that there were choices and paths. Penelope loved herself always, even through being chased around by Welsh Harlequin.

Let me ask you this: Were you born with healthy adult self-esteem, or was however you feel about yourself now acquired through time, experience, and decisions?

It's funny how we brush off a priori knowledge in animals with the word "instinct," like somehow that's a lesser quality, while at the same time striving to invent a way to preload our brains with knowledge through technology. If you're born with knowledge, you're unevolved. If humans invent a way for you to be born with knowledge, you're highly evolved. Go figure.

It's funny, too, how ducks developing a healthy, mature self sense as juveniles is completely overlooked for the intelligence that it is, when it takes a human lifetime for us to maaaaaybe work out one or two of our mommy/daddy issues.

Being as backwards as we are and touting our species as aspirational feels so normal, doesn't it?

That part's not as funny.

***

I can relate to Penelope's stubborn persistence in the face of hostility in certain ways. Growing up I used to worship Michael Jackson. My love for all things MJ began where every White 80s child in the world started: around the time of his *Thriller* album. But wouldn't you know it, I lived in the one town on the planet, Taunton, Massachusetts, where kids my age loathed him. Most kids thought he was gay, which was an open slur back then, even though no one my age knew what *gay* meant. We just knew it was a slur and he was probably gay. I got picked on. I didn't care. I got called gay and all the permutations we thankfully don't throw around so liberally anymore. No matter. Michael Jackson was a god. It was worth it.

I also loved pro wrestling well into the time it wasn't cool anymore. Well past the condescending, "You know it's all fake, right?" era, and just before Stone Cold Steve Austin and The Rock made it cool again. I got picked on for bad taste. Didn't care. Who needed to date in college anyway?

I wasn't all teflon like Penelope, though. I did have body shame issues when I began to balloon up after my parents separated back in third grade. I got made fun of for being fat pretty much always. I was street smart enough to maneuver through the trolls looking for a fight in school by going with the joke and developing a keen self-effacing sense of humor. This helped me dodge the Michael Jackson and wrestling shots, too, but they never stuck in my psyche like the fat jokes.

That said, don't feel too badly for me. I was a jerk to fatter people and pretty much all of my friends. Insults as a form of everyday communication is an art form developed in Massachusetts long before any of us. We're talking about a state where, "Don't be such a pussy," spoken one way is an insult; spoken another is an inspirational speech. Massholes know the difference. And we weaponize it.

On the paranormal side of my life, the same high school friends who made fun of my poorly-fed McBelly never once guffawed at the fact that I thought I was an alien abductee. That was a curious win for me. My family, on the other hand, was not so supportive. That stung.

When it came to that, I was never really sure how much of what was happening with me was real. I struggled with the reality that I might be crazy, but I didn't think what I was experiencing was so easily dismissed. Part of what bothered me about my family's attitude was that I couldn't be sure they were wrong and they were absolutely certain they were right. How could they feel so clear about a subject so murky?

Tellingly, when it came to the so-called spiritual awakenings that overtook my adult life in my late 20s, it didn't matter at all to me whether anyone believed them or not because they actually were clear. No, more than clear, they were clarity itself. They were mysterious, but not in the "Is this happening or not? If so, what are they?" ways of alien abductions. More like, "Wow! So *this* is what we are! What else are we?"

Intrinsic to waking reality is the understanding that sleeping people cannot understand what they're not dreaming. Whereas the argument over aliens is an argument over an external intelligence that may or may not exist, and, if it does, may be being misinterpreted as aliens, the argument over the spiritual is a one-sided, pointless argument. It's like arguing that adulthood exists to children, most of whom believe they are already adults.

Penelope never had to grapple with anything like this amongst her brood. Although, now that I think of it, you could argue that Welsh Harlequin was merely playing dress up while she was born the adult. I wonder if she has empathy for him.

Doubt it. She loves getting him in trouble with me too much. She probably thinks he deserves it. He's such a pussy.

And that, believe it or not, is the branching story of self-actualization. Some animals are born into self-actualization. Other animals, like us, only become self-actualized when the self sense is at its holistically healthiest, whatever that means in one's society. Probably it means outrageous therapy bills. However, unlike any other animal I am aware of, we don't end there unless we stay there. For those adults who haven't dulled their sense of wonder into oblivion, an infinitely larger sense of being is available, but with this cautionary note: your sense of wonder may drop you right back into your normal sense of being if you focus on any one new aspect of your expanded awareness as if it's a power for you, separate from you.

Religious and psychic thrill rides abound in the theme park of mind. Some may promise the death of self, but they will never deliver. Au contraire, you will take a low-paying job as their operator. Spiritual seek-and-find is a lot like self-actualization in that it is a reforming of self, not its death. And only death of self brings a whole new life—one that Penelope isn't interested in because she's satisfied being perfectly duck. One you might be interested in, though, because it's how you become perfectly you. Interested in, that is, until you hear the part about how being perfectly you requires you to not exist. That's when the wall of disinterest pops right up, high as the sky.

Take the wall down for a sec. Just see the obviousness of this. We admit that we are imperfect all the time. And we say there is no such thing as perfection. That means we're not just imperfect, we are incurably so. We are imperfection itself.

Who the hell wants to be imperfection? Not you. So you go searching for spiritual perfection. It should be self-evident that you cannot attain perfection if you are imperfection incarnate, but somehow that fact never quite makes it to your inner monologue and you go looking for it anyway. Anytime you add what you think is perfection to yourself it becomes you, not you it. You'd think that would be a clue to stop, but it isn't.

On you go, seeking that which can never be found and covering it up by telling all of your nonjudgmental friends you've culled to validate you that it's about the journey, not the destination. For your sake, it had better be. You wouldn't want to waste your life trapped in delusion would you?

You seek perfection elsewhere, quit in a huff, claim you found it and work in a spiritual system that appeals to you for the rest of your days, or claim that you are it. Then, maybe, you sell your fraudulent claims to the next seeker of perfection. Maybe you become a famous stop on the road to enlightenment for others.

Yeah, that sounds like you, all right. Some of you. I mean obviously I don't mean all of you, just the ones who are offended.

Say, if you're a fraud, and it was this easy to make a name for yourself, what does that tell you about all the other spiritual leaders you admired?

Never mind. On you go. It's about the journey... Its about the journey....

Clearly the only chance imperfection has at being perfection is to see the futility of all this. I mean really see it. Not see it in disappointment because all this seeking isn't working—but to understand the totality of the problem. The movement of the cycle and why it exists beyond my cynical jokes.

Seeing the totality of the problem so deeply that there are no arguments, no rationalizations, no toddling away from the fact or to an answer, ends the problem. That's it. Seeing it, not doing anything about what you're seeing, because that moment of complete clarity brings the seeking self to a halt. That clarity, that moment, is out of time. Out of the stream of human consciousness. Out of the noise of the psyche. Off the ride.

That timeless moment is Silence, which has just become you. As we discovered earlier, that Silence is living. That Silence is intelligence. And that Silence is perfection.

Silence is you when you're not honking and meeping.

Silence is you when you're not running to and from acceptance and conformity.

Silence is you when you're not trapped in the game of finding yourself or claiming that you have.

Silence is you when you are not.

Caramel & White

This morning Carol called me to the window off of the back lanai. "You have to see this!"

What we saw was the duck run. In the duck run sat Caramel & White in a large dog kennel we had borrowed from a neighbor to keep her separated from her brother and sisters at night so that she could remain among them without them taste-testing her specialized foods and medicated drink.

What else we saw was really surprising: all of her duck family had surrounded the kennel. They seemed to be in quiet discussion with her, taking turns walking up to the metal wire door. It was as if they were saying their goodbyes. Carol said it first, but it was obvious. That's what they were doing.

Ducks have an ingrained wisdom about them that cartoons and bibles have made easy to ignore. Definitely Welsh Harlequin would have given her another reprieve from the sweet, sweet lovin' on this day. This day of paying his respects.

Seeing Caramel & White so depleted that she could not walk didn't exactly give me hope that she'd survive whatever mysterious ailment was killing her, but it did mean that I'd be able to touch her. She disliked human touch, but she was too weak to protest. It was likely that I would have to touch her sporadically if I was going to heal her.

When I say that *I* was going to heal her, it's really an inconvenience of language. We don't have the words to describe the stage of being upon which I slouch because most of us do not live here. Never has a fact felt so arrogant to write, but there it is. And it gets worse.

It is not I who heal. It is I who drop the will of the body and allow choiceless right action to come to the fore. The Will of Silence performs whatever the correct, healthy action is for any given circumstance. I may direct it, may ask for help, but it's going to do what needs to be done whether I know what that is or not, and whether I want it to be that or not. Sometimes it takes a long, obscure route to healing. Sometimes it heals a more pressing ailment instead.

In this case, today, with Caramel & White, what I asked was for this energy to either heal her or help her pass away—whichever was the right thing to do in this moment. I wanted her to live, of course, but part of me feared that all I was really doing was giving her just enough lifeline to prolong her agony. Another part of me realized that I didn't actually know if she was in agony or if she needed the time to say her goodbyes and die on her own terms.

Just yesterday we asked a friend to come mercy kill her, but we backed out at the last moment because she showed signs of strength. Signs that felt like a distant memory today. Even so, the Will of Silence had once worked through this body to ease a finch from the brink of death. Caramel & White's death was not a forgone conclusion.

I knew of miracles.

I knew of miracles through the body typically and erroneously called "My body."

The sun had risen. I was ready to spend as long as it took prancing around the duck run, doing invisible things.

In her near-death haze, Caramel & White was a story of triumphant return waiting to be born.

Chapter 8
Duckie Diets

Our ducks are fat. At least that's what our human friends tell us. To Carol and me they look healthy. As hyper people go, they are contented for sure, but not lethargic. This is because we feed them a breakfast and dinner consisting of fermented grains topped off with a variety of herbs and other organic greens, and let them wander around eating whatever else it is they eat all day. Beetles and cockroaches, mostly. You're welcome.

Some days we feed them snacks in the noontime: dried grubs by the handful or frozen peas tossed in the pool. They also have a little dish of crushed oyster shell. Once in a while we alternate, filling the dish with their own egg shells. This helps the girls get their calcium. Without it, their shells deliver soft and deficient.

Too much calcium will kill a drake. It would take months of chowing down on the stuff, but a lot of calcium ends in tragedy for them. And ya know who knows this? Welsh Harlequin. He won't touch either type of shell.

We keep a pile of grit for them, but they barely touch it. From what I gather, beetles and cockroaches practically roll down their throats. No need to chug rocks when the ride's so smooth.

Again, you're welcome.

There aren't many poisons in the yard disguised as food that will kill the ducks, but avocados will. Their run is partially situated beneath an avocado tree canopy. Had I know they could die eating those when I positioned it there, I'd have never. However, they've been living there for years without incident. The fruit doesn't fall into their run and they are disinterested in the leaves.

Some varieties of mushroom can kill ducks, too. There are even poisonous lookalikes to the edible versions. Whenever I see one where The Goonies roam I'll uproot and toss it, just in case. They seem to know not to peck at shrooms, but why risk it?

Humans have the same reactions to mushrooms: some are food; some are poison. And, famously, we've got the bonus mushroom: some are magic. I wonder if ducks also eat magic mushrooms that transport them to imaginal fantasy lands or render the world they're in askew. If they do they haven't bragged about it to me that I have deciphered. I'm still not as fluent in Quack as I'd like to be.

If they did eat them, though, and had a positive experience—maybe one with godlike mallards and blissful sensations—would they assume they gained spiritual enlightenment? Would they claim to have had the Will of Silence activated?

I think it would be hard for bliss to have an effect on such naturally joyful beings. That bliss sensation would really have to be working in overdrive. But also, I do speak enough Quack to know that they aren't concerned with seeing through illusion. I take that to mean they already do.

***

There was a time early on in Paratopia history when my broadcast partner and I decided to do magic mushrooms to see if that psychedelic journey could produce the same or similar effects as those we experienced in the poorly-named "alien abductions" we had both experienced at points throughout our lives. We had read and heard accounts of people encountering aliens on such journeys involving various substances, psilocybin mushrooms being one of them, and so we had to find out for ourselves. We were like scientists, but high.

To that end, we had our own separate mushroom adventures, what with Jeff living in Maryland and I in New York. And at different dose levels, too. Jeff only ate a few caps; I ate two heaping cupped handfuls at once like a starving Penelope eats a termite mound. Anything for science.

I don't know where Jeff scored his mind-bending salad fixings, but I acquired mine from a good friend in Manhattan. I remember that he was excited for me to be doing this because I had never done drugs and didn't drink. I think he got a kick out of corrupting me. As he was bagging the dried shrooms, his wife shot him a brow-raised look of, *You're crazy giving him so much*, and said pretty much that. She said what he had bagged would be enough to blow my mind. He laughed and added more.

However much that was, that's how much I did. Very scientific, indeed.

Heroic dose in hand, I decided to take some precautions. Famed psychonaut Terrence McKenna once said that doing shrooms is unlike any other hallucinogen in that a pizza delivery person could come to your door and you could snap out of it long enough to pay him, get your pizza, and then go right back into the trip. Sounded to me like he was saying shrooms leave you lucid enough to not get lost in illusion and hurt yourself, but nothing works as advertised, so I decided to hide the cutlery. In my hallucinogenic stupor I wouldn't want to see a knife as a banana and decide to peel and eat it. I didn't know if shrooms would give me the munchies the way pot was infamous for, I just knew that most people threw them up shortly after taking them. Surely that would leave me hungry, no?

I took my trip alone, which you're not supposed to do, in my apartment in Queens, when I was advised to be outdoors. It was nighttime, which I'm sure someone told me was a mistake. I had a secret weapon, though, that none of these critics had counted on: the Jackson 5's greatest hits CD. Nothing bad can happen when the Jackson 5 is playing, right?

Sure, sure, The Grateful Dead and Pink Floyd made music specifically for this moment. But the Jackson 5 immediately put you in a good mood. Or me, anyway. And it was my mind that I was blowing. That other music may be fine for taking a couple of mushroom caps to chill out to some music and a pretty light show that spills into the room from behind your eyelids, but this was not going to be that. So I put the Jackson 5 CD on repeat and sat cross-legged on my bed, propped up by the wall. There I waited. And waited.

My friend who gave me the cow pie miracle drugs did warn me that they would take a while to kick in, but it took longer than I expected—around 45 minutes—before I felt anything. All that time I expected to hurl. I had a little garbage can by the bed just in case I couldn't make it to the bathroom. I found normal mushrooms to taste gross but these dried shrooms were next-level offensive to my palate. Yet and still I kept them down.

When my 45 minutes of normalcy were up, the Jackson 5 began to sound like the soundtrack to a horror movie. The music was bending and slowing down. The voices got deeper and molasses-like, as if a serial killer who wanted me to know he was in the house had slowed down my record player. There were no longer gleeful, fear-repelling pop sounds bouncing out of my speakers— these were Giggles the Clown dancing around his basement, modeling his favorite skin shawl, noises.

I very quickly scuttled into the living room and turned off the Jackson 5, then retreated to my bed and sat up cross-legged again. I receded into a meditative state allowing the Will of Silence to come to the foreground. I thought this was my ace in the hole, as it were. I didn't need a shaman or a guide. I suspected the Intelligence of Silence would know how to navigate the craziness to come. Mercifully, it did. For ten full hours.

The unrelenting night was just revving up.

***

When the visuals began to kick in, what I initially saw with eyes closed was a series of violet, rounded symbols flashing through my mind. These were like a barrier that only a high dose of shrooms could pierce to get to the outlandish trip. I found that out months later in my second and final trip of any kind when I took just two caps to experience the difference. Same soft, violet symbols, but nothing after that. This time, however, I broke through and into a vision of animated tie-dye mandalas spinning gyroscopically. It felt like these animated artworks would never stop and I found them disappointing. I wasn't a huge tie-dye fan, but at least I now knew where the hippies got their artistic vision from.

I don't remember much of what I experienced that night because the events, whether in the room or in my mind's eye, roared over one another like ocean waves in a storm. I do remember, though, that in the beginning, I had two voices narrating everything I was experiencing seconds before I experienced it. One voice was my own, as if relaying these events to my Paratopia audience, which I intended to do if I survived this, and the other was Terrence McKenna. They sounded like recordings that didn't compete with, so much as compliment, each other. And then there was conscious, unrecorded me—a tiny voice in the back of my own existence, squeaking out, "Help!"

Eventually I broke through the *Welcome To Hinduism* symbolic showcase at the third-eye EPCOT center and leaped into a whole other ride. Gone were the narrators. Now I was inhabited by the voice of a carny barker/used car salesman type of pseudo-being whom I took to be the mushroom entity. It was me physically speaking to myself but putting on a funny voice. Anytime I'd get scared, the mushroom entity persona would say, "Awe, come on! It's not so bad! This is awesome!" And I'd agree in my own voice like a giddy stoner kid, "You're right! This *is* awesome!" Then I'd be thrust into some other plane of existence, a blue Krishna consciousness space, or fly to a pyramid in a grassy field on another planet, and feel joy and astonishment and deep connection with whatever was happening.

Or should I say, pseudo-joy and connection. Yes. Yes, I should. I'll tell you why in a bit. Now, I need to tell you what the Will of Silence was up to this whole time. It was positioning the fingers of both hands in the "OK" sign and expertly "playing" energy centers up and down the front of my body. There was no music involved but I could see chakras lighting up with each placement of my hands. I looked like a Kenny G concert and arguably sounded like one. I intuitively knew what this was for and it was nothing so bland: the Will of Silence was weaving me in and out of the immersive virtual realities that would take up most of my night.

Eyes open told a much different story than eyes closed. The close-eyed visuals came in waves, and I could tell when I was about to ride the next one because it was foretold by a chugging sensation in the body. Perhaps this was an exaggerated feeling of blood pumping through veins. It was akin to what I've described through the years of sometimes feeling a chugging in the head before sleep, which always foretold nightmares. What that chugging is I don't know, but it is physiological.

Back to the chugging of the shroom, I'd get a break between inner journeys where I was lucid enough to feel the creeping fear that I'd eaten too much fungus and was now broken like this forever. How would I explain it to my family? What garbled mess of ideas would pour out of my mouth if I tried? I was afraid I had gone insane.

With eyes closed I was fully in it, whatever it was, like a lucid dream. There was no room in inner space for fear. Eyes open, on the other hand, I had plenty of room to think and therefore fear. But I also had two allies of sorts and a rational tether to normalcy. My main ally was a thin elephant's trunk that peeled off of a shadow cast by the window curtain to my left. He stayed by my side the entire night. For some reason I found that long, silent snout hanging in the air next to my face comforting.

Aside from my elephant buddy, there was an ally that seemed like it should be an enemy. For the duration of the trip, my apartment was covered in thick, green vines with rounded, non-menacing thorns, which were red in color. Not just the apartment, though. When lying on my back, there was a vine growing inside me. It began in the stomach and snaked its path all the way up and slightly out of my throat. While this made it difficult to breathe, it also helped me in a way. It became my second tether to reality as it forced me to concentrate on breathing. I had to keep my breaths steady, even when I was scared, because I felt as though I was choking on this vine. The problem of the vine, like everything else in the room, disappeared the moment the mushroom engine chugged alive and thrust me into a new eyes-closed visionary excursion. But there it was, back with everything else, when I returned. It begged the question, If these hallucinations were comprised of random, unconscious material spilling into the room, why did they have better continuity than dreams?

Between the Will of Silence moderating my nonphysical experience and being forced to breathe steadily as a physical experience, I think I held myself together fairly well. But what really quelled the rising fear for me was a simple act that became my rational tether to normal reality for the rest of the night: I knocked on the wall behind my head and there was a wall to knock on.

You always hear these claims in psychedelia that the hallucinations aren't merely illusions caused by the active chemical psilocybin, but are a combination of out of body experiences, astral travels, spiritual enlightenment, and a peek into other dimensions. Reality is an illusion, my fellow travelers assure us. And so I decided to test that theory. Unpaid scientist once more, I knocked on the wall.

Know what my knuckles didn't touch? Vine.

Know what they did touch? Wall.

I knocked on the wall, and the wall was the wall. This was a huge revelation for me in the moment. Even through the hallucination of the vine and my suspicion that my hand might go through the wall. the wall still existed. There was solidity there. A reality there. And so I thought, 'Okay. I'm going to get through this because it isn't real.'

Then, because I was high, I thought, 'Wait, what if I can walk through the wall, though?' To my mind in that state trying to walk through the wall was the only way to prove that consensus reality was the illusion and psychedelics provided a trip to the really real. There to prevent me from acting on the question, however, was the carny barker mushroom voice coming out of my mouth. "Well, why would you want to do that? This is awesome!" he assured me.

"You're right! This is awesome," I agreed like a gleeful little boy. Rational mood swing having melted back into the awesomeness of whatever "this" was, I closed my eyes and flew to another spiritual plane in the underbelly of the universe.

***

I had to get to the bathroom and I had to proceed with caution, just like the street signs warn. Although I was of normal enough consciousness where maybe I could answer the door if I had ordered a pizza like bard McKenna said, I was also of normal enough consciousness to worry that if I planted my feet on the floor, I might hallucinate myself falling into a bottomless pit, while in reality I'd have somehow broken my ankles. Like, when I snapped out of the spell of the mushroom would I be lying on the carpet in need of medical attention?

I set my worries aside because I had a more pressing issue pressing on my bladder. I tempted the Fates and gingerly stepped one foot at a time onto the floor. It felt marshy, like walking on soft earth. That I could handle. Bottomless pit? Woulda been more trying.

So I was okay. Great. I could stumble carefully through my now crooked apartment. I found that all the rooms were slanted like an amusement park funhouse. Doorframes and bookcases sloped drastically to their left. Everything was covered in that thick, green vine with the blunt, red thorns. My place had become a cartoon jungle within the concrete jungle of New York.

I tripped my way the few steps it took to make it to the doorframe between bedroom and living room. This place was a farce. I was a farce. Gone was McKenna's voice. Silenced was the mushroom entity. Now, I spoke and emoted with a new character. There was still normal me in the background, a pipsqueak of a voice, but in the foreground this satirically dramatic, clownish entity spoke. Are we sensing a theme here?

Crap, was I turning into Giggles the Clown?!

I vividly remember standing in the doorframe, propping myself up for balance, and bursting into laughter. Then, like an animated Warner Bros. cat burglar, I slapped my hands over my mouth and shifted my eyes left to right as if I might wake a sleeping giant. I followed this by throwing my right index finger into the air and proclaiming, "This is serious!" Then I slapped my hands over my mouth again as if those words had accidentally escaped me. Every moment of being up and about was this absurd. I was the absurdity and I was calling attention to the absurdity, the absurdity of being a concerned, fearful adult, and the absurdity of this whole hallucinogenic situation.

Stumbling doorframe to doorframe like a man escaping a sinking ship, I eventually made it to the bathroom. The bathroom was all jungle, no different than any other room. And the toilet itself was made of a long, hollow vine spiraling down seemingly into infinity. There was that bottomless pit I worried about.

I used the toilet just fine. No surprises on the floor when I came to the next morning. In the moment, I decided to stay out of bed. I thought maybe it would help me snap out of this, so I bumbled over to the living room couch and turn on the TV. I had no issues working the remote. Perhaps this was coming to a close!

I don't remember the time, maybe midnight or thereabouts. Whatever channel the TV was on was playing the movie *Apocalypse Now*. Though the television was a 1080p plasma, the image had horizontal lines running throughout like an old cathode ray TV. Now playing was a scene where people were going down a river in a boat. They looked demonic. They had big black eyes and pinched, bird-like faces. I sat on the couch cross-legged, which is not how I normally sit, and, again, was over-emoting in an absurd manner. "Mm-hmm... mm-hmm... yup... mm-hmm," I commented to everything that was going on in the scene. It was as if this clownish version of me were doing an impression of an adult pretending to understand and enjoy *Apocalypse Now*, which is arguably how all adults watch that movie.

I very quickly had enough of clown-me pretending to be engrossed by television, so I turned it off and went back into my bedroom. I must've switched on a light because I decided to look in the full length mirror, which my friend who gave me the shrooms warned me to never do. He said a universally nightmarish visual reflects back at you. I had avoided the mirror over the bathroom sink, but I decided to look into this one just to see what the universal hubbub was about.

Like a typical White person in a horror movie I felt the privilege kicking in. I'd be the one to survive the preternatural nightmare of my reflection because *reasons*. So I gazed at myself in the mirror and saw my... my....

Wait, was this my true face? Was I also a black-eyed, pinched-face, bird-like demon, like the cast of *Apocalypse Now*? Because that's what I saw. And my body was a pudgy, absurdist clown body. I was an animalistic clown having an enlightenment experience while trapped in a psychotic delusion. Just in case I had any concerns about that, cartoonish clown-me blurted out, "Yep, that looks about right! Let's go see what's out the window."

I penguin-waddled over to the window and peered past the fire escape. Couldn't see much more than outlines of buildings in the night, but, man, was there ever a lot of traffic noise and bird song. Neither made any sense given how residential this area was and that it was past midnight. Heck, the window wasn't even facing the street. Nevertheless, there were all the bustling sounds of midday happening out there, except for one more odd element: all of the sounds were playing backwards. Engines idling, trucks and cars rolling down Metropolitan Avenue—even the birds were chirping in reverse.

My out-loud reaction as this demonic bird clown? "Yep, that's interesting. That's not as interesting as this. Let's lie back down here."

Hey, as clowns go, at least I really wasn't that sadistic Giggles of my comedic callback. I picture him in white clown makeup and full costume. My face looked distorted, but I wasn't wearing any makeup or costume when I checked the mirror. "Clown" was more the vibe of who I was and the place I was in. It was how I carried myself and the goofiness of my voice saying goofy things.

Now I was wondering why I kept saying this stuff out loud. Whose voice was this? Why was this happening?

I did a lot of muttering to myself at times. Things like, "Did you hear that? What was that?" Not in the clown voice, but in my own. However, it didn't feel like me saying it. And as I pondered this I had a flash of myself as this bird clown in a bathrobe sitting cross-legged in a chair on the fire escape as if it were a porch. I was going through the motions of reading a newspaper and drinking coffee in the morning.

Again I was struck paranoid by the thought, 'Oh, God, is this what I am? Like, is this another dimension where I am this being?' But I immediately chased the forming fear off with a rational deduction that even though this place is all jungly, the building is still the building. If these animalistic bird clowns are a people, they aren't capable of constructing this apartment complex. And if their living here is dependent upon construction workers in our dimension having built it, well, that makes no sense. So this critter that I am can't possibly be real. This all has to be part of the hallucination.

I don't know if it was in reaction to that revelation or something else, maybe nothing else, but I immediately roared with uncontrollable laughter straight out of the scene in *Evil Dead 2* where the main character, "Ash," is sitting in the living room of a demon-haunted cabin having a psychotic break. In the scene, all the stuffed animal heads on the wall, books on the shelf, light on the table—everything in the room with him becomes animated, laughing at him. And then there's this fisheye lens warping his face as he belts out, "Baaaa-haaaa-haaaa!" Abandoning sanity is all he can do to escape himself.

That's what I was doing, minus the animated room. Sure, there was my elephant trunk pal hanging from the curtain, but he remained stoic in the face of my insanity.

I fell back onto my bed and lay there screaming laughter at the top of my lungs. My face felt as though it were split into four equal quadrants, each one squirming in a different direction as I laughed. Behind the involuntary performance lay me worried that I was going to wake my neighbors, and further worried that they were going to call the police who would kick in the door and haul me off to a mental hospital.

Thank the gods for New Yorkers. Everyone was used to lunatics. People tended to keep to themselves and go on with their lives. I could have been being murdered, and no one would call anyone.

Then again, there was a pretty good chance I wasn't making a sound, just imagining it. Whichever was the case, this night refused to end and I had not encountered aliens, which was the main reason I had dared myself into taking this hyper bewildering trip in the first place.

I told the carny barker mushroom entity that I wanted to see aliens. That's what I was here for. "Awwwwwwwe," he said in mock concern. Then, "Why would you want to see that? That's boring. This is awesome!"

"You're right," I agreed. "This is awesome!" On I went to the next inner adventure. But when it was over and my eyes opened and I was staring at the ceiling, something was barging through it. I heard clunking and crashing as though a metallic contraption was busting through the roof of the building and then the ceiling of my apartment, which it did. Yes, that's right, a small spaceship partially crashed through my ceiling and got stuck in it. Ask and ye shall receive. It looked metallic and organic, like it were a living, breathing, old timey machine with gears made primarily of the jungle vine my apartment had been consumed by. Small grasshopper people hopped out to assess the damage.

Next thing I knew, my body was being pressed down six feet under soil. I was being buried alive in dirt by an invisible force. I swiveled my head to the right and was greeted by a grasshopper. He plink-plinked his giant eyes at me and chirped like a cricket. All of that played out in jittery stop-motion animation style. This, uh, UFO crash with insectoid aliens was as close as I got to having an alien abduction. I doubt Congress will call me up to blow the whistle on this one.

I'm not certain what happened next, but this occurred some time after, and it may have been next: lying there with my eyes open, I watched a cartoon procession of white musical notes marching by right to left in front of my face. They were formed by the sounds outside, real or imagined, and by any noise in the apartment, including me shifting in bed. Every new sound added to their song with new notes marching into the line. At one point I swallowed and the high, tinny sound of saliva in the back of my throat produced a note that marched out of my right ear and into the musical parade. I was mesmerized by this for however long it lasted.

Time. That was *definitely* an illusion.

***

10 hours later, I was seeing octopus tentacles. Every time I shut my eyes, a mass of squirming octopus tentacles. I hadn't slept at all. Apparently, of all the impossible things I could experience on shrooms, sleep was a bridge too far. Every time I tried to nod off the Will of Silence jerked my head awake. Thanks for that.

Slowly but surely I was finally emerging from this wackadoodle headspace. The visuals were reduced to those tentacles writhing behind my eyelids and, with eyes open, jagged shadows by the closet creeping across the bedroom. For some unknown reason, those shadows scared me, which prompted me to jump out of bed and pace around the living room for a bit. I could walk normally now, but I wasn't fully out of the mushroom's grip, which again brought me to the fear that I was stuck like this and would need to be institutionalized as a madman the second I tried to hold a normal conversation with another human being.

My fear was unfounded. I did fully emerge late in the 10th hour. However, a few days later, now in a beachfront cottage on Cape Cod, Massachusetts, I had the magic mushroom equivalent of an acid flashback. This happened at night. I was crashing my mother and sister's vacation rental, sleeping poorly on the couch in the living room, when I was awakened by the sound of sirens, red lights flashing in the window, and police officers rushing door to door looking for someone. They started banging on our front door and yelling for us to open up. I gazed out the sliding glass doors in front of me, which overlooked the Atlantic Ocean, and saw that the water was lined with trees on either side of my sightline. Hovering in the center was a silver disk-shaped craft.

Aliens. Finally.

Except I knew there shouldn't be trees in the ocean. And I knew nobody was reacting to the loud insistence of the cops. Nice try, acid flashback—I knew this wasn't real. And when I pondered the entirety of my hallucinations, along with what I'd learned about other types of inner voyages later, I realized that psychedelics and plant medicines had more to tell me about so-called spiritual experiences than alien or paranormal ones Another brilliant deduction by yours truly considering how pretty much everyone in psychedelia has been preaching this for decades. It's part and parcel to the claim that such trips induce various forms of out-of-body travel. I mean it's kinda what the word *trip* implies, right?

Having traveled thus, thanks to the magic of the mushroom, and having also experienced the authentically spiritual, which drugs cannot touch, I can tell you that I get it. I get why so many people believe that experiences like these are Truth or provide ultimate enlightenment. But they ain't it.

See, when we're talking about Truth we're talking about Ultimate Intelligence, which is not a construct of thought. Such intelligence is only apparent in the absence of thought. Not just apparent, but living through the body as its self-awareness when the brain has stopped projecting its thinker. You remember me writing that a buncha times throughout this book, right? Well, I'm writing it again.

From our vantage point, this is the union of unlimited awareness with the limitations of form and time. For this merger to take place there must be a moment where thought ceases. A moment of silence. A moment of nothing. Which I forgot to capitalize. Here: a moment of Silence. A moment of Nothing.

One major aspect that all drug and plant journeys share is that they are noise. There's not a moment of Nothing between them. You may become a quiet, tiny witness in the background of the stuff happening up front, but you're never not there.

My shroom trip speaks to a variety of states and stages of noise. There was no moment of Nothing from which the noise sprang. It was like being trapped in the hyperactive imagination of a clever being with attention deficit disorder.

It's not that there weren't good feelings involved, by the way. I know I concentrated on feeling fear and paranoia in my accounting, but those were when I came to something of normal lucidity or recognized my voice in the background of an unstoppable torrent of outlandishness upfront—the reverse mullet of conscious awareness, if you will: business in the back, party up front. No, mainly what I felt were good feelings and wonderment, but with an undertone of frustration. Frustration at how inauthentic all of these allegedly more real than 3-D reality experiences were. As I've explained elsewhere, the difference between this and authentic "enlightenment" is the difference between understanding a great, multifaceted joke and tickle torture. Both will have you rolling on the floor with laughter, but one flowers through understanding and the other is forced upon you whether you like it or not.

And that's what this is. It's a facsimile of the real. "The real" being that which transcends and includes the universe. Visiting other planes of existence, floating inside Krishna consciousness... these are all within the field of the known. They are thought constructs. They are formless aspects of the universe itself. And they are enlightening to the extent that they point to you not being the one imagining these imaginative places you feel like you're visiting. They are enlightening to the extent that you feel at one with the universe. They are enlightening to the extent that they instill in you the understanding that there is more to life than materiality. But they do not transcend and include the universe. They draw you deeper into its possibilities. This may feel freeing but it's actually a replica of freedom. You are never free from thought here.

What you are is subsumed in other forms of it that at once feel foreign and familiar.

No, there is no moment of Nothing here, no cessation of self. Just the recontextualization of self. Self as putty. Self as background static. No selfless moment.

There are replicas of Nothing, though. People have reported what they claim is an experience of Nothing. Most whom I have seen said it was depressing or terrifying as they found themselves alone in a void. Some people liked being alone in the void, but all were, in fact, aware of themselves as existing and aware of the void as a thing they were in. And, obviously, they had a feeling about it. That ain't Nothing, that's something. Three things, in fact —the witness, the feeling, and the space they occupy.

I'm not saying these are bad things to experience. They're not. Many, perhaps most, people find a lot of good in these experiences and grow from them. Arguably, that's what they're here for. We will explore all of this in greater detail in chapter 22. For now, just hear me when I say that growth is not the transformation we need. Personal evolution is not Silence. And we need to be Silence. Desperately. Look around at all that the world of noise hath wrought. Earth is overrun with human noise made manifest. We continue to invent so many of the ideas that pop into our heads nonstop that the world is a bit too claustrophobic now even for us.

Think we can go on like this for much longer?

Will Earth let us?

***

People who know such things from experience assure me I had a bad trip. Of course I don't know what to compare it to since I haven't done any other drugs, but to me it wasn't bad. It just wasn't *it*. It wasn't, well, it wasn't the abduction experience for one—but more importantly for this book, it wasn't the Will of Silence. Clearly. The Will of Silence knew how to navigate it. Being trapped in Toontown from *Who Framed Roger Rabbit* for 10 hours was spectacular in its own right.

When I told my friend who dealt me the shrooms of my adventures, I was as exasperated at what had gone on as anyone who experiences something like this for the first time. "What do you think this is? I mean, you think we're journeying to other places? Do you think it's all in the mind? What do you think is happening there?" I asked him.

My friend, who has only ever taken a few mushroom caps at a time to watch the pretty colors while listening to music, responded confidently, "Oh, it's food poisoning."

Once again, the ducks are way ahead of us.

Chapter 9
Duck Ninjas, Stealth Pigs, Bionic Cats

Ducks are highly intelligent people and therefore highly curious. When they were younger, most times when I cleaned their run or did any yard work I would randomly turn around and be startled by the band of eight standing behind me quietly with their heads bobbing about their elongated necks. They were trying to figure out what I was up to. They looked like how humans look when we stand on our tiptoes trying to see over the heads of other people in a crowd. It's that same movement.

These ducks are so loud and proud, flappy and fast-running, that their ninja skills seem out of character when they use them. Like us, ducks have the ability to shift gears when they need to. Sometimes they waddle and you hear them brushing through the grass. And sometimes they appear as if out of a cloaking device. No wasted motion. No sound. Just there. Lurking. Assessing. Adorable sprites.

It's not just ducks. Wild boar tromp through the yard all the time. Until they don't. Until they decide not to sound like a thundering herd rolling down the mountain. Until I turn around, and there one is, feet away, staring at me in an otherworldly manner.

Free roaming pigs are not the lazy, fat slobs we create on farms. From pigs to cows to dogs, everything we tame we turn into the worst of us. Still, that doesn't answer how massive, fast-running pigs can sneak up on us in the wild. Perhaps they learned it from elephants. Have you ever seen footage of an elephant stepping into the jungle as if in slow motion?

Elephant. Tall and wide.

Jungle. Densely-packed trees and assorted greenery.

Silent? Completely silent? Not even a stubbed toe? How?

The whole scene feels preternatural. Even the way they move. It's as if they have more frames in their movie than we do. Like we move at 24 frames per second and they move at 120. Probably because they are using every bit of their musculature to its peak ability, which makes their movements fluid as cats.

Speaking of which, we have three cats. Our toothless hunter is named *Sir Palm Trees*. He loves spotting baby geckos crawling around the ceiling and alerting us to them because he knows Carol or I will bust out the yardstick to guide the little fellas down and, if we're lucky, into our hands. Then we can put them outside.

Our unlucky times, which are many, are Sir Palm Trees's lucky days. These are the times when the lizards decide to jump for it. Unless they land on us they're going to land on the floor and into the hell that is kitty cat playtime. Or the jaws of hell if Sir Palm Trees wants a snack. (More like gums of hell in Sir Palm Trees's case. He only has his front canines.)

Nowadays, Sir Palm Trees is contented with catching the critters and meowing for one of us to pick them up—but here's the thing about that: he pins these zippy little lizards effortlessly, yet he doesn't appear to be moving any faster than I am. He just drops his paw on them. But when I try to drop my paw on them, if I am at all successful, it will usually take several attempts. Geckos are just too fast for me even though I look like I'm move at the same rate as Sir Palm Trees. I must not be, but my eyes can't pick up the difference.

***

For thousands of years we Westernized humans have been hoodwinking ourselves into believing we are living in the penthouse suit in the skyscraper of life, special and alone. Unfortunately for us, the skyscraper is a tower of babble—it's all hot air. But it's *our* hot air and that's what's important to us, which is why the plain-as-day observations about life and Nature that indigenous peoples already understand come as sets of unfolding revelations to us. Because we are set on being unique and controlling in our biblically-ordained position as the only valid observers on Earth, we have a hard time observing Nature without twisting what's there regardless of us into an exotic revelation for our social or personal evolution.

The reality is, breathtaking discoveries like, *Ducks have inner lives*, and, *Pigs can outwit me*, are not new. What's new is Westernized Man's vision peeking out from behind the biblical blindfold. The blindfold that has written in bold lettering on its inside, facing our eyes, **"Animals and plants are dumb creatures God put here for us to do with as we please because we're special and above them. They're not alive like we are."** It's the blindfold that Christian society tied to our heads at birth whether we were born into a Christian family or not, Jewish family or not, Muslim family or not, religious family or not.

But there are moments. Moments of sight. Moments of clarity about animal intelligence. Sometimes these moments come accidentally, sometimes through effort. In these moments the equality of other beings, along with their showing us what we give up to claim we are above them, overwhelms our blinding delusion of grandeur. The slightest glimpse at their greatness reveals our smallness. The top of a pyramid is always smallest.

What, now, is learning?
What, then, is living?
What is evolving?
What are we?

II

A.D.
After Ducks

"You were wild once. Don't let them tame you."
                                    - Isadora Duncan

Chapter 10
A Honu World

Let us start off the *A.D.: After Ducks* section with a story from before. Before Carol and I had ducks. Before there was a Carol and I. It's the story of the first time I ever snorkeled alone in Kahalu'u Bay, Hawaii, back in 2012.

Like most places on Hawaii Island, Kahalu'u Bay is deceivingly mysterious, magical, and mercurial. All the M words. Currently, it is a tourist trap of a beach due to its prime location on Ali'i Drive in Kona, and also to its unique two-sidedness. Facing the ocean you notice that the right side is wide open. This side is home to enough moderate wave action that it's a great place for learning how to surf. The left side is an amazing safe space for swimmers, children, and snorkelers alike. It is full of fish and blossoming coral, and, while not shark-proof, is shark-resistant. What makes it so is the stone breakwater running roughly half the length of the bay. It cuts off where the surfing half begins. It is here, in this bay, where I was first initiated into the mysteries of the shallow sea.

I met my initiator in 2012 when I surfaced on the shoreline, retiring from my first day of snorkeling as an official resident of Hawaii. I had snorkeled in Kealakekua Bay with a friend who took me out a number of years prior during my one and only visit. Back then I was assessed by a pod of spinner dolphins and given the go-ahead to keep swimming. Now a full-time wannabe local,

I planned on being a full-time sea creature. This was my first of many solo snorkeling adventures.

I didn't know all of what awaited in the bay, but I was hoping to spot a honu—a Hawaiian sea turtle. I didn't. However, what I discovered in bright, colorful fish completely mesmerized me. Some were small and cute; some were large enough to eat me. Some were munching on coral and some were floating around enjoying a lazy afternoon. I was fine with having missed out on turtles. Time to go home.

I swam up the inlet and began peeling off my fins when a stranger, a White man, sitting on a concrete wall along the shoreline, started yelling at me. I could barely hear him over the crashing waves, but he was definitely yelling at me and fiercely pointing at something.

I hollered back, "What? ... What?" I was trying to understand him and thought he was saying, "Turtle!"

No sooner had I relayed, "I don't see it," than this big ol' sea turtle swam up into my lap. The honu patted my belly with her flippers and checked out my fins and snorkel mask, which I was holding in my hand at this point.

I knew enough to immediately throw my hands in the air while she checked me out because there was a lifeguard on duty, watching, and it's illegal to touch sea turtles. I gave my hands to the sky and said, "I'm not doing this!"

Please don't fine me! Please don't haul me to jail!

When the honu was done assessing me she slid back into the ocean and swam away. That was my first meeting with her people. It felt like an acceptance into the ocean by a gatekeeper who was clearly meeting me as an equal, not a chance encounter with a dumb animal living in a lower tenement of Western civilization's tower of babble. My new friend in the green carapace didn't stumble into my lap by accident. She was a humbling welcome committee of one who was curious about me and ultimately accepting of me.

There is a saying here that Hawaii accepts or rejects you, and it's true. There are many trials, many ways. This was one of them. The honu assessed me. The honu left. That was it. And it began my lasting relationship with the honu people.

Since that encounter, wherever I swam around the island I encountered them, often in dramatic fashion. One time, while snorkeling in Kealakekua Bay, a honu friend popped up from below me, seemingly out of nowhere. Side by side we swam for maybe thirty seconds and then we both surfaced for air. As we were swimming, he turned and regarded me with that stoic honu face. That face of silence and centuries. That face of recognition and kinship.

I remember telling coworkers who were not Hawaiian about the first encounter. To a person they said that the honu gatekeeper was my aumakua. And to a person they thought *aumakua* was the Hawaiian word for *spirit animal*, which means an animal that appears in your life to welcome and protect you. It's your go-to guardian, which sounds cool and all. I like sea turtles. A bit slow in an emergency land situation, but why not? It felt right. It felt like all of that was going on—the welcoming and the protecting. And then later in speaking to Hawaiians I found out that, no, this definition of aumakua was wrong. *Spirit animal* is more of a self-involved bastardization of aumakua than anything.

Aumakua really means an ancestral protector— someone from your family who has died and taken the form of an animal or a rock or some other natural being to guide and protect the family. Since I'm not Hawaiian it stands to reason that I don't have Hawaiian ancestors. I doubt I have ancestors from anywhere, to be honest, as I'm not in touch with my ancestral human past at all. Rootless, I don't expect ghosts from my bloodline to be hanging out, itching to help me. And yet here come the honu doing just that. Acting as guardians. Not guardians of me, though—guardians of the sea. Protectors of Hawaiian waters potentially *from* me. I was judged to be okay. One of the good ones. I'm now allowed into the sea as a friend.

I think that is closer to the truth. Sea turtles don't need to protect outsiders, they need protection from us.

And here's another thing about honu: they don't care about our laws. They define the terms of our relationship unless we block out their full aliveness and deny their equality. Only when we do that may we selfishly define the terms of our relationship, which usually revolve around how abusive we feel we can be toward them, whether or not they're food, or if we want to build a structure on the sands where they breed.

The honu sea keeper doesn't care that by swimming into my lap I could potentially get in trouble with the law. Nor does she care about me getting the cultural definition of aumakua wrong. Doesn't care that I'm not Hawaiian. Doesn't care if I'm culturally ignorant or simply uneducated. Doesn't care what I call her. Honu just wants to make certain that I am a friend of the sea. If I keep the sea safe she will keep me safe in return. That's a living animal relative connection, not a dead human one. Not a spirit animal vagary.

It's also a Hawaiian one, because beneath the rational is the magical. Both are alive here. I experience both. The magical is as real as anything defined by Western science, even though Western science is ill-equipped to identify it on its own terms. However, I know enough not to culturally appropriate any ceremonies, chants, or teachings about Hawaiian magic because I cannot understand magic in the Hawaiian way. It is not engrained in me as one who is genetically and culturally tied to Hawaii.

Let's be simple and say that Hawaii is living. And the ways in which Hawaii communes with us are myriad. Sometimes they are natural and sometimes supernatural. Let's pay homage to author Jeffrey J. Kripal who first split that compound word into *super natural* to emphasize the natural part. The super natural is natural here. It's a part of everyday life. Gods and goddesses rule. Ancestors abound. As one elder casually told me when I first arrived, the dead roam the Walmart parking lot at night. She meant it.

I'll give you two more extremely different examples of the obvious natural magic oozing like lava from this island. The first occurred as I was embarking on a long, treacherous hike into Pololū Valley. From every vantage point atop and within, Pololū Valley reveals itself to be one of the most jaw-droppingly gorgeous places on Earth. It is not untouched by the corrosive force of tourism, but it is one of the lesser-touched places mainly due to the fact that the only way into the valley is on foot, and the hike down is a winding path of hazards and missteps waiting to make your acquaintance. It's made all the more perilous by the fact that there is no guardrail. You could take a tumble that is your last.

Still, if you play it safe and take it slow you will be fine, provided you're in shape enough to make it down a mountain and back up. Though I look like the fat guy who would take a tumble that is my last, I am just barely in shape enough to make a day of it and not have a stroke. I was in no better shape—arguably in worse—back in 2012, on my inaugural descent into the Valley with a friend visiting from the mainland.

As we began the trek I heard a voice in my head. It was male. It was me and it wasn't me at the same time. I realize this sounds strikingly similar to both the mushroom entity and the clown that I became during my shroom trip, but this was different.

I had heard this voice a few times before, all relating to Hawaii, though not all in Hawaii, so it didn't come as a shock that such a paradoxical speaker would exist in my head. The first time I heard it was when I was living in New York. I was outside, walking the streets of Forest Hills, and for the first time seriously contemplating a move to The Big Island. I looked up at the buildings that defined the sky and thought about how much I would miss the sense of depth they create. Then this me/not-me man in my head told me I wouldn't miss them because there are buildings in Hawaii. Moreover, the skyscrapers that wow me here will be replaced by tall trees, mountains, and lush forests. I won't miss a thing. My sense of wow factor and wonder will transfer onto Nature, essentially.

The other handful of times I heard this voice occurred after I made the no-turning-back decision to move here. I had moments of creeping doubt, but the voice swooped in to assuage my fears, telling me how I will truly feel, not what I imagine I'll feel, once I go.

If the me/not-me voice is actually just me dissociating or something like that it's curious that it only began with Hawaii. Back in the 1990s when I had committed to moving to New York City straight out of college, I was scared because I had a minor phobia of big cities. I was raised in Massachusetts and the thought of visiting

Boston made my stomach churn ever since I was a wee child. I knew nothing about life in New York except the awful crime drama of movies and television. If ever there was a moment for a schizoid voice to psyche me up for a move it was this one.

Nobody said nothin'.

Turns out I was wrong about New York, though. I ended up loving the Big Apple right from the start. Perhaps no one in my mind assured me I'd love it because I was moving there with my sister and so I had her as a security blanket—or at the very least an inmate to commiserate with if it turned out to be the open-air prison I was imaging—but I think it's something more. Something we'll get to later in the chapter.

Now at the head of the Pololū Valley trail, the paradoxical voice in my head instructed me to do something I would never tell myself to do: "Take off your shoes and run down the path."

I protested in my head that this was the dumbest idea I never had because I would surely wreck my feet on jagged lava boulders that had fallen onto the path over time. Or a massive, snaking tree root. Or slip on a wet surface like "Sliding" Billy Watson on a banana peel and pratfall my way to the valley floor.

The me-ish voice responded decisively, "Do it. You'll be okay. Just take off your shoes and run down the path."

We argued a bit like that and then I caved. I stopped, stripped off my shoes and socks, and took the dare. I ran. And by that I mean *walked briskly and with purpose.* I wasn't exactly hurdling in the 2012 Summer Olympics, let's put it that way.

I immediately found that the voice was right: my feet knew exactly where to go. I had an instant superpower of being nimble and quick on the rough and raw wilderness path. It was as if my shoes had been holding me back this whole time. It was also as if I had been holding me back this whole time with my uneducated decisions on where to place my feet next. Anytime I would try to take control of my feet with what I thought was a better way to go—a shorter distance in a forking path, or a less treacherous stone to leap to—I would trip, stub my toe, or land on the sharp end of a jagged rock. Mercifully, no pratfalls ensued, but the lessons learned were that shortcuts aren't always the best cuts—in fact they may give you cuts—and thought gets in the way of choiceless right action.

So much for the glory of free will. Feet in conversation with Earth provide better instruction than me navigating a place I've never been.

Having made it down the mountain I wanted to put my socks and shoes back on to explore the Pololū Valley floor. Its black sand beach, freshwater stream, and pine tree forest beckoned. Those stiff, brown pine needles covering the forest floor looked unforgiving, but that voice of mine/not-mine insisted, "Walk on the pine needles. Don't worry about it. It will be painful, but it will only be painful for a little bit and then you'll get used to it. Furthermore, pain is just a sensation, so just think about it as another sensation, not something that hurts."

Realizing I would never use "furthermore" in a sentence to myself, I did as instructed and kept my shoes off the entire time. I even kept them off for the walk back up to the car. It was a full day of *earthing*, as the bohemian kids called it.

I made it down and back in one piece. The me/not-me inner voice was right: I survived the impossible sprint. And I was right, too: my feet were throbbing masses of fleshy hurt for the next few days. It felt amazing in the moment and I felt accomplished—but man, oh, man was I in pain afterwards.

Some years later, too late to be synchronistic, I came across a documentary about the Rarámuri people of Chihuahua, Mexico. These folks run up and down mountains at ridiculous speeds for long periods of time as part of their daily routine. Westerners wonder how they do it. They don't, I realized as I was watching the doc, their feet do. They trust their feet enough not to get in the way. And part of trusting their feet is trusting Earth. It's like being a great dancer. Great dancers never count their steps because they're not actually dancers, they are the dance. That was me that day: hippo in a tutu from *Fantasia*.

In Pololū Valley I was the valley walking itself. When I stopped being the valley, when I put those shoes back on and drove to the Westernized pollution oasis I called home, is when my feet revealed themselves to be bloated, blistered wrecks. My tootsies didn't have to adjust to walking Earth. They had to readjust to being padded against Earth, floating within rubber, foam, and fabric, ironically, for greater comfort and arch support.

So that was a lesson in super nature.

Another complimentary lesson was learning who the not-me part of the me/not-me voice was. It was Earth. Perhaps, specifically, Hawaii Island.

I mean, it truly is all me in that I'm not channeling an entity or suffering a personality disorder. But I am used to being a brainiac of a person, a separate self divorced from all of our natural interconnectivity. A Westerner. An American. A White guy. At that point in my life, however, I had already shed my separate-self discomfort and moved to heart. I was in a sense living a bilingual life. I could speak both brain and heart languages. But I was new to heart, and in heart is where Nature speaks.

Nature may speak to you through animals like the honu. Nature may also speak through you as you, as with the land, which is what happened here. If I were brought up in a natural culture like the Rarámuri, I doubt I would experience a voice. Earth and I would be an integrated fabric of decision-making. There would only be right action in the moment of running barefoot, and I would be that action. I wouldn't need to be talked into allowing it to happen.

What natural cultures do, which we may also do when we live fully immersed in that state, is speak Nature. They speak Nature because they identify as such. They are not just "at one with Nature," as the cliché goes, but are actually *one*. It's not a decision. There is no interval of thought about it and no being proud of your epiphany that animals and plants are people, too.

That said, Nature and I were not one in Pololū Valley. I still had a bit of internal distance from Nature and so I heard a voice that was mine but not mine, which reflected that division. Hawaiians speak Hawaii as Hawaii speaks Hawaiians. I speak *with* Hawaii and Hawaii speaks *with* me. That's the best way I can describe all of this.

See how thought obfuscates the way of the actual?

See how living conceptually is not living at all?

***

My second example of communing with Hawaii is a little less real-world and a little more goofy. What follows may fairly be described as a waking hallucination, which took place in April, 2014. I know the date because I blogged about it. This is what I wrote. Poorly. What are ya gonna do? It's a blog....

    I was awakened really early by a woman's voice. It was probably the crack of dawn but I was too out of it with the tired to check my clock. I just heard this woman talking. She kind of sounded like one of my roommates. I have two, both female. They have real bedrooms. I have a dining room converted into a bedroom, which means that where a wall and a door should be there is a bookcase and a curtain. I hear everything. It sucks. But don't cry for me Argentina, because while you're stuck in Argentina, I live in paradise.

    Except paradise comes with a severe cost—one worse than dining-bedroom. That cost? Feral chickens who never know what time it is.

    Rrr-r-rrr-r-rrrrrr! at all hours of the day with these friggen roosters. The only time of day they can agree on is crack of dawn. That's when they're like, "TIME TO GET UP! HEY, EVERYBODY! TIME TO GET UP! REMEMBER MIDNIGHT? FALSE ALARM! NOW GET UP!"

    Rrr-r-rrr-r-rrrrrr!

    Many are the mornings when I slog out of bed and chase them out of the yard rattling a rake and cursing these loud, shrill, atonal opera singers. As I type, I hear two of them crooning right now. But distantly. They aren't in the yard. In fact, they haven't been in the yard since the morning I heard that woman talking. Now back to that....

The voice is not my roommate's after all. Is one of 'em watching TV? Are they up this early? What time is it?

I listen closely. Finally, I can make out what she is saying. She's saying, "Not bad... Not bad.... That's not bad... Not bad...." over and over. I realize it's not a roommate, not the TV... holy crap!—Is there someone in the house? Or do we have a ghost?

Now I'm lying there scared listening to this. I'm still half asleep and not attempting to get up. I'm like asleep but paranoid. It's weird. And then it gets weirder for I hear this woman's voice saying, "That's not bad" morph into *"Rrr-r-rrr-r-rrrrrr!"*

That's right, I am hallucinating, turning the distant call of a rooster into a woman's voice. And I realize this at that moment, that very tired-yet-alert-enough-to-be-paranoid moment. And as incongruent as this all is, it gets *incongruentier*, to... make up a word. I actually find myself saying to the rooster chick, "No, it's not bad, Pele. But I can still hear them."

See, even though I know I am hallucinating a woman's voice over a distant rooster, I am also still in the middle of hallucinating. And so, me, in the middle of hallucinating, believes that the woman is the Hawaiian volcano goddess Pele and that Pele took time out of her busy morning to come to my apartment and use her magic to keep the chickens a safe distance from the yard so that I may sleep. And now she's saying to me, "See? That's not so bad." Like, *Look, I'll make sure the chickens stay away from your window so you can sleep.*

And me, always one to look a gift horse in the mouth—I'm whining that it isn't good enough. But, because it's Pele and she's a goddess and I'm living on her turf, I'm whimpering with all due respect.

Anyway, I thought that was interesting, especially given that the chickens really have stayed away from the yard for the last few days. When I'd rattle a rake at them, it just emboldened them. I think they came back in the mornings for their daily chase. Honestly, I think they kinda liked it because they would come right up to the window and *Rrr-r-rrr-r-rrrrrr!* for as long as it took to respond with a chase. Sometimes I'd wait a half hour, forty-five minutes, just to see if they'd go away. No such luck. Then I'd chase 'em and they'd shut up. So who were they talking to if not me?

Whelp, at least now we'll have what esteemed doctor Tyler Kokjohn calls "scientific proof" that Pele is real or not. If the chickens stay away, she's real and I'm turning into Hank Wesselman. If they come back, she's not and I'm turning into the man who mistook his wife for a hat. Yup, that's science.

Years later I told a Hawaiian friend who is a Pele worshipper this story. She said, "That's not Pele. I don't know who that is but it's not Pele." According to my friend, the real goddess, as opposed to the popularized version, is a "powerful bitch" and does not manifest like that. I know goddess energy when I see it, but not when I hear it, apparently.

This experience along with the Pololū Valley voice and the honu greeting in Kahalu'u Bay share a fundamental unspoken message with the female voice of alien abductions, as well as the coordinated involuntary movements from the Will of Silence. It's a Secret of Silence that we already learned with the honu guardian: they do not care what we call them.

I may not believe I have ancestors who act as intermediaries, and I may not worship goddesses, but they don't seem to mind. They keep on keeping on with me no matter what I believe about them. Perhaps they've taken pity on me.

Hawaii has definitely taken me under her wing and for that I am beyond grateful. I am dedicating my life to here and so now we share the natural language of apprenticeship. It's the language of learning for learning's sake, not learning to become something. I move in the world as the world moves me. This is true for all of us when you think about it. The difference is that both Earth and I are conscious communicators. Sometimes.

I mean, me? Sometimes. Earth? Always.

Such communication, such wholly conscious movement, is a part of Love with a capital L. Love, which encompasses all. Not poetically, but actually. Not personally, but impersonally. Impersonal Love transcends and includes the communication, the movement, the poetic, the actual, and the personal. It is all. Love is all. Love is Truth. You've heard it before. You've sang along to it. It's a trite cliché. It is also the fact beyond facts, Love is. Therefore, so is forgiveness. It's baked in.

Earth forgiving my drifting in and out of conscious communication is as instantaneous as understanding why I do it. That gem of a character flaw is for me to sit with. You've got your own. In fact, character flaws may be the only things you truly own because you can't give them away. But you can see you as you actually are. When that happens, the character drops and the miserable play you've been acting in ends.

When the miserable play ends, life becomes... play.

Chapter 11
The Secret Death of Trees

In November 2022 the volcano on which my family and I live, Mauna Loa, erupted. About a week and a half prior I was making my way along the winding wood chip path to our gazebo where I do most of my meditating. And by *meditating* I mean setting my sense of personal self aside for the Will of Silence to come alive, flow through the body, and will it to do whatever is appropriate for my own best health, and the well-being of the environment around me, in that moment. On this day I came to a long-dead bleached bush in the path, which I probably shouldn't have let grow there in the first place. The weather got droughty and it died.

I plucked it, threw it into the wind, and said to it, "Be free." The notoriously strong Ka Lae wind had a funnier idea, pushing back at my notion of freedom by dropping it in the same spot it had been all along. We're just like that, people are. When we're set free, we tend to stay in our familiar routine.

A bit later, the wind picked up and that dead bush became more like a tumbleweed. Because I'm a fan of irony, I thought, 'Finally free. But not alive to enjoy it.' And that's us, too. Not necessarily fans of irony, but in a number of other ways that's us. We do, after all, live in a society that pats itself on the back for its written-down paper freedoms that often don't apply equally to its citizens in practice. And we worship money as the ultimate paper god. Paper is power here. Literacy and agreements. We're free on paper. But *are* we free? Or are we slaves to the grave, as the saying goes?

As I watched my new tumbleweed friend make a break for it I imagined it settling into a pile of bushy bones made from others of its kind. And then I imagined that one day the sun would burn them in their dry, decayed state. This pile of bush bones would become fire. Fire, which is their next stage of living.

They aren't really just dead and gone, these old bones. They're dead and waiting to be reborn as fire, or else turned into mulch and dirt to become fertile soil for others to grow in. In death they are life nonetheless. In death they are truly alive and completely free, for death is life, and life without death is a rich man's goal generated by fear.

My stream of consciousness thinking brought me to the California wildfires. Why does Nature make wildfires?

The obvious answer is to make room for new trees and plants, but it's also because certain of them necessarily need to experience being fire. Dead trees hold a kind of life force in stasis within them that requires lighting up for them to become enlightened. Is such fiery transition felt not as burning torture but a transcendental celebration for what is, by all appearances, dead wood living anew?

It is in my imagination. I hope reality, too.

But then what of the surrounding young and alive trees getting cooked before their time? Surely to them wildfires are tragic. They've not gone through the death process. And the fire feels like, well, fire. They must be in pain because they have pain receptors that the dead trees quite properly do not. If you're a tree burning before your time it must hurt like hell. The only good that comes of your sacrifice is for other trees to see this and be aware that they are also secretly fire. And, one hopes, to learn the lesson that to be set ablaze before your time is to be tortured, not enlightened. Therefore the only preparation to be fire is death. Now we're ready to go deeper into the Will of Silence.

***

As I recounted in my book *Urgency.* and elsewhere, I had a moment when my brain understood that the personal self sense it was projecting—namely Jeremy—was a thought construct blocking out Truth. In that moment the brain stopped projecting me. I died while the body remained alive, and after a brief bit of nothingness the brain turned me back on. With me flowed a new and mysterious friend, an energy that, like Penelope in her culture, is much abused in ours. As Imua showed us earlier, this energy is classically, vaguely, and wrongly defined as a primordial goddess, or goddess-like, feminine energy. One that lies dormant, coiled at the base of the spine. If you figure out how to trigger it, or it triggers on its own, it rises and either spiritually enlightens you or drives you psychotic. And it is likely, the stories go, that you will feel all sorts of physical pain, extreme heat, extreme cold, psychic attacks—lot's of fun stuff—along the way.

It is true that in our initial meeting said energy rose up the spine, just like in all the stories. Everything after that? Not so much.

As it rose it blew out my back. Not in the cool *union with the universe* way so many people educated on the subject believe is waiting for them to experience when their immortal essence explodes out the top of their skulls, but in the, "Oh, that sucks" way of it slipping two discs in my back. This happened because I was (and remain) physically out of shape, which is what thin people call round people like me, so let's go with it. Also, I had a propensity for slipping disks. I had pulled off this feat a few times in my adult years, though I didn't know enough about it to name the problem. In those moments I would feel a jiggle in my spine, an organ slide out of place, and it hurt. Later that day or the next, whatever the organ was would slip back into place. I assumed that would repeat here, so I foolishly let it linger and pretty much did every awful thing one can imagine to make it worse. It was my ignorance that hurt me most.

The point is, when the Will of Silence blew out my back it wasn't a spiritual emergency. It was a physical one. It happened because a fat guy who didn't do any stretches or yoga hadn't the necessary elasticity in the spine for a surge of palpable force to run through.

When I say *force* I don't mean to conjure images of an electricity roaring into the body from some unseen dimension. Nor do I wish to invoke the legend of an energy pool at the base of the spine awaiting activation. It was neither of those. Nor was it snake-like, nor drastic in any of the ways often described. It was fast, I suppose, in that it made it to my head in about a second. When that happened my head started spinning in a circle as if doing a neck exercise.

Fancy that. My body immediately wanted to exercise. Probably it always did, but I was in the way because exercise is for pussies. Pass the nachos.

All of this is to say that for those who claim some universal energy (or Goddess energy) causes them intense physical pain, to the extent that they are not misdiagnosing the cause, it is the pain that comes with lack of preparation. I didn't know I needed to prepare for anything. I was never warned that the death of self was the unblocking of an aliveness that transcends and includes me, so preparation wasn't on my agenda. Nor should it have been.

What we have before us is a crucial paradox about preparation: preparing for this event with exercise or anything else would have prevented the event from happening in the first place. Really, one needs to exercise for the sake of exercising, not because one fantasizes a day when a new energy will blossom in the body whose flow will challenge rusty pipes. It will never flow if you're expecting it to or hoping it will. And I can pretty much guarantee you that the peoples of ancient times who worked with this energy and knew all about it didn't need to be told to get in shape first. Not even a topic of conversation, no sir.

And that's it. That initial unanticipated ascent of energy is the moment where real and awful pain may occur. Or may not. Depending on you. Given this, odds are that when people claim to experience painful symptoms of a spiritual awakening they are not talking about the Will of Silence even if they believe they are. They may believe it based on what others have written or said, but the simple fact is that if there is not a moment of no-self then there is not a moment where this energy may fully, wholly be here. This is why you can't prepare for it. Anticipating a death of self keeps self identity alive. You're now the anticipator.

It's important to remember that there are other energies in you, such as chi, which may be mistaken for the Will of Silence. Chi is the vital life force. It may be manipulated by you and aspects of it may be inadvertently triggered by you. Perhaps this is the name for your pain.

Remember: the crux of the problem is that you, the self-sense of the body, are the blockage that needs to clear out for Truth to come first-person alive in the body. When Truth is wholly alive *as* you, you don't just become a syphon of wisdom. Truth speaks the mind, the body, the psychic, the subtle, the everything. Truth becomes you. If you're still in the way of Truth, and you don't realize that your existence is the problem, I can see how pain may arise when the energy flares. If you are inadvertently triggering chi or some other energy that appears to be dusting off your energy centers, that's a problem since you're ultimately the dust.

Is that clear? Are *you* clear?

I am going to put this as plainly as I know how: Nothingness, Silence, Truth. These are all speaking about Ultimate Intelligence. Ultimate Intelligence is formless, timeless awareness that in simply being is being all forms and all time. You and I are this singular awareness whether we are conscious of it or not. To be conscious of Ultimate Intelligence is to be conscious *as* Ultimate Intelligence. Otherwise we are conscious as ourselves.

Fun fact about Ultimate Intelligence being all forms: some of these forms may project their own seemingly formless awarenesses. Humans are such forms. The human body projects you and you may swear you're a formless awareness wearing a meat suit. However, no matter what you tell yourself, you are a projection of cells in the body. You're a colorful illusion, like a rainbow, caused by material processes. You're fake. Pretty, but fake.

It's the thing back in chapter 2 that Blondie got while you were like, "Huh?"

Sorry, not *it*, you. You are a thought construct. You are psychological time being projected by the brain—the blockage to the self-awareness of timelessness. We've been through this. Now here comes the part even Blondie would find daunting, so pay close attention....

When timelessness becomes time, from your perspective it must look and behave like it is coming in through a specific physical location—the base of your spine in this instance. And it may feel as though there is a blockage located in that spot preventing it. This blockage is like a blood clot comprised not of platelets and fibrin but of you, the defensive thought construct, and the smallest whisper of the Intelligence of Silence. It's like there's this pipe in your back through which flows universal energy when you're not cutting it off like a valve. You can't completely cut it off, though. There's always a drip, drip, drip congealing above your bum-bum.

When you don't realize that this blockage is you—when you see it as an *it*—you may decide to play around with it and manipulate it, ironically, for spiritual gain. Perhaps you have read a book or watched a testimonial from someone who swears that all this amazing spirit stuff occurs when you learn to control it. What they in all their mastery don't know is what you in your novicehood also don't know: you're playing with a clot.

A few pages back I told you that you or your favorite guru may be misdiagnosing energy you sense rising and falling and doing all that fancy psychic stuff. Now the royal we are adding this: it may also be a function of this clot. Specifically a function of blocking out the Intelligence of Silence by defining it as an unalive, mechanical energy that you control. When you block out the Intelligence of Silence's will power for your own as you try to engage it, this is what you get. Hot flash yoga.

Again, the body's noisy self-awareness has to dissolve completely for the Will of Silence to be the case. When that happens the Will of Silence is a permanent fixture. It's not there one day and gone the next. It's there with you, always. When you are silent it is active. When it is silent you are active.

You are partners, at least, and likely more. Likely you two are one. Likely, just as your existence was the denial of it, your existence as an entity partnering with it is blocking out the fact that you are one energy. But that's another likelihood for another time, preferably a timeless time on your own. For now it's enough to say that the relationship is neither one of master and slave nor teacher and student.

If you're not dissolved then all of your mental issues and perhaps your "spiritual" issues, whatever they may be, are going to constantly get triggered. Perhaps it is best put this way: it's a good idea to be physically limber prior to the death of self. Either way, death of self is the only means for this energy to come fully alive in the body. However, if you physically train for your fantasy of a magical moment where you die and the energy wells up, then it will never fully blossom because you're supplanting the real with your own projected conclusion. Even if your conclusion is correct it is in the way. You think you're building toward a union with the real and yet doing anything towards that end creates an illusion. It's like you're too busy trying to achieve your goal of dying to actually get around to dying, you see what I mean?

Likely you will end up playing with the blockage and not know it. That's right: you'll be playing with yourself. And so, when you hear me deriding people who claim to be powerful with the energy, as I am prone to do, if you're like, "Wait, why does this guy think he's had legit experiences and none of these other people have?" it's because there are few people who have actually dissolved their sense of self.

The reason such people are rare is not complex. "You are the universe and the universe is you," to steal Jiddu Krishnamurti's phraseology. He said it to illustrate that all people are psychologically the same and basically unchanged through time. We are all expressions of one human consciousness. I take it a step further and say that you are the universe and the universe is you, *literally*. He knew as much but was smart enough not to have that conversation with people who couldn't even hear the first order predicament. Ironically, the point I am making is a more obvious fact than what he said. You are literally both living in the universe as a person doing stuff and living as the universe, comprised of its matter. You are not separate from the universe no matter how unfathomably large and unknowable it is to you.

Now that I think of it, is the universe really so unknowable? Don't you both want the same basic thing?

The universe wants to remain intact and so do you. However, the universe grows through new experiences, whereas you only appear to. You only appear to because time is an illusion. From the timeless view, everything here is always already happening right now. All of your growth? All of your new experiences? They feel new, feel like they're unfolding. And from your point of view as a speck of life within the universe they might as well be. For most intents and purposes, they are.

However, the death of self is the death of psychological time. Sure, the body is still alive and in time, but the mind is dissolved. And in that dissolution, Truth becomes the mind of the body—timelessness as mind merges with time as body. And that's when you realize you've been going through the motions of newness all your life, but that everything is one energy and timeless and blah, blah, blah, something about ducks.

—Wake up! Stop daydreaming while you read!—

Now. The universe at large is this living, breathing, picture. All of its living and breathing creates the illusion of movement as newness or evolution. But what the universe knows that you don't is that it cannot experience anything new from within itself. The new must come from timelessness.

A person who dies egoically resurfaces with some gold for the universe. The universe converts Truth, amongst other things coming from such a person, into events in time, events within itself. One example of these events is religious paths that anyone seeking Truth may stumble along thinking they're getting to Truth or that they've found it, when what they found is a simulated experience that is so profoundly rich and meaningful to the person that they may have their thirst for Truth quenched for a while. To this end, the universe has set up within you through the butt blockage the ability to have a simulated near-death-of-self experience. This simulated dying/awakening is meant to impress upon you that you've achieved enlightenment so that you will press the issue no further—so that you will still exist, because you existing is the universe existing.

Is this beginning to make sense?

Human consciousness is of the human body. The human body is of the universe. That material-based consciousness dying for this parallel force of immaterial intelligence to arise as you cannot be a permadeath situation. Or so says the universe. The universe doesn't want that transcending energy to be you. You must resurrect, so to speak. You may visit Truth or commune with Truth, but always keep one foot in the human stream. That's what the universe at large wants.

But what do you want?

Conveniently, you want to remain yourself, too. The universe would love nothing more than to bring novel experiences back one at a time to build up its interior domains with imaginative funhouse worlds and the such. And you're the same. You want to bring you with you when you die, somehow, and you want to bring back experiences to either share with people or hoard like a miser. You want to be the one who gains superpowers and moves on through time with them. That's evolution. That's mastery. That's special. You deserve it.

That's all well and dandy except there's another thing that actually needs to happen whether you want it to or not: complete, timeless transformation. Instantaneous mutation out of self, out of psychological time. Not the building of self through desire and acquisition.

Problem is, instant transformation is antithetical to the universe, which is time. It's antithetical to you who are time. The universe's tantrum against death of self is the baby's tantrum against being born. Therefore, so is yours.

Seeing this problem completely includes seeing that you cannot act on it. Seeing triggers the transformation on its own, and it is here where you become a Secret of Silence: timelessness is secretly, deeply you and is also the universe, for timelessness transcends and includes time. Nothingness transcends and includes thingness.

Truth transcends and includes the universe, and you are now all of that statement.

***

We of the Westernized mentality believe that we own the universe. We think we are masters of our domain. And we're wrong. Just sit with the implications of your mentality being completely wrong for a moment by yourself. Not in a group. Not talk to anyone else about it. Be with you.

Sitting with the entirety of the problem and getting it deeply enough that the brain projecting you sees it without you coloring it, comparing it to similar ideas you've learned, jogging your memory for that perfect quote of wisdom from some ancient sage that best encapsulates it, bending it to your furtherance, is the moment the brain turns you off. What happens next?

We always want to know what's next, don't we? We seek that assurance of our continuity above all else. But seeking continuity as we're discussing our ending poses a bit of a quandary, don't you think?

That doesn't mean I'll keep it from you. I won't.

Next, you may learn a thing or two more about the Will of Silence from direct experience. Until then you're just guessing and playing with other people's ideas. After you finish this book, don't add mine to the list. Be with you.

You can read books, watch videos, and look at signs and symptoms of awakening that other people talk about breathlessly. Maybe you've had a couple of those alleged symptoms and figure you must already be an awakened one. But that's like turning to PubMed with the sniffles and concluding you have diphtheria.

You ever do that? Okay, not necessarily with diphtheria, but like, you know, turned to a medical dictionary to define symptoms you're experiencing of an illness where you're thinking, 'Oh, God. I'm dying.' And the reality is, just because you have some symptoms doesn't mean you're dying. Or in the case of awakening universal energy, doesn't mean you've had the death of self.

Be with you.

There can be no authority in this. I am telling you this forcefully, and although what I'm saying is correct and true, I cannot be your authority because you can't know that you can trust me. Perhaps, then, it is best to trust what I am conveying only insofar as it brings you to a place where you will explore this further within yourself, not to a place where you believe me and go on with life or disbelieve me and go on with life. I could be wrong. I could be lying. Find out for yourself.

That's the important point: if this intrigues you at all, find out for yourself. The first step in finding out is not at all intuitive. It is a Secret of Silence we've already touched on: you have to abandon your sense of intrigue. You have to do away with the search and the wanting to search, the wanting for an answer, the wanting for whatever it is that brought you here in the first place. You have to see that desire is now in the way and desire, any desire, is you. You are the thing you're doing. You are desire itself. And you have to ask yourself why it is that you are the lust for enlightenment and why it is that you're in the way.

Really. Go ahead and ask yourself those two questions. Be with you.

Getting this intellectually doesn't mean it's easy to do. It's not easy to get rid of that desire, because it's you. You are not a person desiring, you are desire. You are seeking. You are your function.

You're like a little truffle hog sniffing out truffles. Yeah, that's you. And now you want the ultimate truffle, that deep down in the earth truffle. And someone who has been leading you along by your piggy snout says, "Oh, you want that ultimate truffle? Well, you've got to stop being a truffle hog for that."

Oh. How do I do that?

Then you go on your merry way sniffing out answers when the answer is, that snout of yours cannot touch the ultimate truffle. It can sniff out all the other truffles in the world. You may feast on them until you're fat and happy, but not this one.

Your piggy brain must see this and stop projecting the hog for that ultimate truffle to appear, because you obviously cannot dig it out. The truffle digs itself out, you dig?

Digs itself out. Truffle. Pig. That's my analogy. Wacky world we live in, huh? But there you are.

So, yeah: don't believe anyone. They're not helping you. They're not doing you any favors when they say there's a super electricity in the spine undiscovered by science or that everyone's got it and it is the primordial force behind the universe. Your reaction to this news is supposed to be what? Something like, *Oh, great! I must be humming with this heroic energy right now! I need to learn what all of my superpowers are so I can teach them like the master of the universe I was born to be!*

And then you go on, roaring down the road of life in your shiny, new enlightenment narcissism with the terrible muffler, and we all keep destroying everything together.

You want the real, you've got to be the real. Stop doing for the sake of stopping, which means the brain hearing this and getting this, and that's it. The Silence that ensues isn't just the absence of your noise. It isn't just quiet. It is intelligence per se. That Intelligence of Silence moves the body and you are that.

Remember this: we are fire. We don't wield fire, we *are* fire. Anything less is someone blowing smoke up your tailbone to steer you toward their favorite tasty truffle.

Remember also that because we are fire, your back may burn like fire if you're not limber enough to handle rising energy. Whether by the invisible hand of celestial forces barely understood by us or the lending of a hand by me to Penelope, the good contains the bad. In the pursuit of stillness, try not to get crushed behind a doghouse.

Best way to do that?

Only way to do that?

Stop pursuing all tales of spiritual enlightenment and religious security, and don't then run away from pursuing them because you think that's what "Stop pursuing" means.

Be with you.

Chapter 12
Cuddle Fish:
The Longest Beach Day

Beach day!

Let's head back to Kahalu'u Bay and talk story about fish. This bay is full of them. It's like a rainbow coalition of fish. Including the rainbow fish, funny enough. When I first moved to Hawaii this was my favorite place to snorkel. It helped that there was a food truck on the beach selling shave ice, a staple of the Hawaiian diet. What helped more was the up close and personal time available with so many swimming beings from fish to eels to turtles.

Physically, fish couldn't be more different to us. They might as well be aliens. Maybe that's why we call ocean dwellers *sea creatures*. Ever heard of land creatures? Air creatures? No. Because they're not alien enough.

And yet even sea creatures have the same wants and needs as we. They love to eat. They love to poop. They love to poop and then turn around and eat it. They also love affection. They will even accept it from higher beings like humans because they know what we don't: we are not higher, we're equals. Let's wind our way to that fact with some adorable true stories from my life, shall we?

I grew up a husky teen eating crap. Crap far worse than shave ice. Not literal crap, mind you, but still about on par with fish eating their own turds. This set the tone for my adulthood as a fat guy eating more crap, including shave ice.

In 2010 I magically woke up a vegetarian. Literally it was that. I woke up and the body had dropped its taste for meat. I had nothing to do with the decision. However, from a nutritional standpoint I was a wee bit tepid about being vegetarian because I knew I needed protein, was too lazy to cook anything that took too long, and didn't know if I could find crap, or meat-crap substitutes, that would appease my crap palate. All of that the case, I decided I would keep eating fish and eggs. Eggs don't count, I figured, because they're not alive. And fish don't feel, so what do they care?

I still feel that way about eggs. Fish? Not at all. My god are we a callous people. We'll tell ourselves anything to do what we want. Fish have nervous systems. They feel. They have a life drive. They want to live. And they have emotional lives. They are relatable. We're just going to have to deal with that and be grateful for their lives when we take them to eat them.

I mean not me, you. You'll have to do that. I gave up fish about a year after moving to Hawaii because I didn't want my snorkel buddies to smell their relatives on my skin and fear me. I didn't know if they smelled or sensed me as a fish-eating predator, but these were my undersea pals now, and you don't eat your pals.

My ploy worked. Some of the usually shy, standoffish tropical fish allowed me to come closer to them. And the more social species swam right up to me and let me pet them. I won't tell you which species wanted to be cuddled because I don't trust you. I don't know if you've been honu-approved. Also because I met a local artist who had the tip of her right pinky finger chewed off by a fish. This is why you should always keep your hands folded behind your back when observing the life of the sea unless you're going to pet them. Which you aren't because I won't tell you which ones.

I don't trust you.

***

It may be that learning has no ceiling. There certainly seems to be no end to it. Not for me. Not for you. Not for fish. Well, maybe for fish. But they already know the basics. They don't second guess the basics the way we do. Like, for example, before when I said we're equals and they know it? We may suppose we're higher because we think about them in so many different ways that they would find it baffling if they had the ability to find our thoughts baffling in the first place. We say such differences make us more complex and therefore higher than fish on the ol' consciousness hierarchy, but that's just a story we invented to be able to call them *food* or *sport or lab animals* and not think twice about taking their lives or torturing them.

Fish know we're not better than them. The fact is so obvious as to not even be pondered by them. It's an engrained fact. Only an incredibly naive species would assume that their ability to kill and eat another animal—or wipe their kind out of existence completely—makes them higher beings. Fish can be brutal to their prey, too. That doesn't make them higher or lower, does it?

We think that our ability to ponder from different angles, which entails living in confusion, and to extinguish all life at the press of a button we invented to do just that places us high atop Earth's chain of being. This is as backwards as archeologists finding that early homo sapiens and neanderthals were more evolved than we gave them credit for because recent discoveries show that they were artists who performed rituals and buried their dead. What this actually tells us is that we have not fundamentally evolved in hundreds of thousands of years. We're silly in our denial of how far we haven't come. Fish see it. They see us. They shrug us off. Shrug their tiny fishy shoulders. "Pet me."

Learning has no ceiling because there is always more to discover. Also, because ours is a partial mind that we naively prop up as the pinnacle of earthly evolution (or godly will), and so we're always going to be confused, self-soothing ego strokers. We're always going to react, not act. Always going to put at least a second's hesitation between ourselves and reaction as we consider what to do next. We lack the ability to directly act when necessary except in emergencies where the decider takes a back seat to reflexive response. This confusional glitch, like all the other misuses of thought, is pridefully referred to as *human nature*.

When you boil learning down crudely like a Maine lobster, it is taking in information to either build upon or reject so as to build upon something else. But what about consciousness itself? The consciousness underlying the learner? We've heard a lot about higher and higher stages of consciousness. Is there a ceiling there or does the hierarchy go on forever like learning?

Turns out consciousness is different. Awareness per se does have a ceiling. Clarity, when it one hundred percent zaps confusion out of existence, brings us all to the same understanding. It floats us to the ceiling in one gravity-defying epiphany. There we may meet others bobbing along the chandelier. Others whom we may have perceived as spiritual masters or even aliens reaching down to lend a hand, drawing us to that gaudy light.

When we get there we realize it's consciousness all the way down and that down is up is side to side. There is no hierarchy after all. The confinement of the room with its ceiling and really stupid-looking chandelier—what the hell is that thing doing there anyway?—is an illusion.

No one was reaching down to us after all. They were waving *hi* and we grabbed their hand. We made it awkward. Now, we're all partying on the ceiling like *Mary Poppins*.

We're not higher beings reaching down to the fish, is my point. Well, my nearly lost first point. We're reaching over to the fish who are swimming across to us, receptive to relationship. Again, fish know this already. They're already perfectly fish in the way that we are *not* perfectly human. The only thing we perfectly do is pretend that imperfection is our gift, and friction is what affords us the ability to imagine further and grow and evolve.

Evolve. Riiiight. That's why we so easily relate to the thoughts, emotions, and actions laid out in the *Epic of Gilgamesh* written some 4,000 years ago. Because we've... changed?

The difference in human consciousness between now and 4,000 years ago lies in how we've reconfigured our physical and psychological limitations. This includes you who think I don't mean you. You who read a book like this and feel it doesn't apply to you because you've read something similar elsewhere and so, having previously trained your eyes upon words like these and comprehended them, believe you've been freed. Freed from the limitation that is you. As if freedom from your own repression is a mere cognitive exercise. As if freedom from thought can be gotten to by thinking about it.

Thinking is not freedom. It isn't limitless energy. The thinker is very much a defined circumference. When that bubble pops, one is truly free and not actually floating to the ceiling. And, again, this includes well-read "free spirit" types who don't blunder over these concepts because they've read them so many times that the very act of verbal comprehension tricked them into dreaming they were fully awake as is—not like the rest of us sheepshead fish who mistake the aquarium for the ocean. They can have their bubble pop, too, it just takes an extra prick. May I be that prick for you.

That said, you will probably never be as conscious as cuttlefish. I have zero faith in that for any of us.

Chapter 13
Cuddle Fish II:
Electric Boog-eel-loo

Have you ever seen cuttlefish up close in person? Holy moly, are they a trip!

Cuttlefish are cephalopods that not only change color to camouflage themselves, but also their shape and texture. Swimming above them as they traverse the ocean floor, one is treated to a psychedelic show: their bodies instantaneously morphing into whatever is below them while they roam. You can find science articles addressing how smart they are. How they change color to reflect their moods. How they hypnotize their prey. How they can delay gratification by giving up the food in front of them for the promise of something more delicious later, which only humans and chimps had been observed doing until recently. And how they sometimes transfigure into the opposite sex to get laid like republican congressmen.

I once saw cuttlefish in Kahalu'u Bay do something else extraordinary. Something I haven't read an article on. Of course I did, I am me. Regardless, this is no big fish tale....

I wasn't snorkeling alone. I was with another witness, the sister of one of my roommates at the time who was visiting from the mainland. We were floating on the ocean's surface watching a cuttlefish who got a little spooked by us and responded by quickly laying down flat, like a sand dollar, and camouflaging against the beige rocky bottom. Neat. We lingered perhaps a bit too long for cuttlefish comfort, for within seconds another cuttlefish swooped in fast and lay on top of him or her. Protector to the rescue!

One camouflaging cuttlefish trying to hide the other camouflaging cuttlefish tilted both of their camouflaging organs. They went berserk, rapidly changing all sorts of colors, unable to read each other. We thought it might drive them insane so we left. These were not fish who wanted us to pet them.

***

I didn't quite get there, but I was almost *that* friend. Nearly everyone's got *that* friend who has a life-changing spiritual epiphany that they respond to by drastically transforming themselves. I mean beyond the behavioral change required by the idea involved. They buy different clothing. They maybe listen to different music. Enjoy new smells in their home. Perhaps they start surrounding themselves with new friends they think will understand them better because the newbies are currently going through, or have already gone through, a similar life change.

That friend's reaction to what they think is a new spiritual height isn't on par with, say, quitting their job and working someplace else, or buying a new home and moving to a new town. Their personas, their interests, their sense of style—a whole lot changes with the felt spiritual epiphany. When we see this we often think of cult leaders who force their followers to abandon their families, to wear certain garbs, to develop a community amongst themselves, and to block out the rest of the world. Or we think of gurus and spiritual teachers who encourage similar breaks with people and habits but aren't militant about it. Whoever we think of, they all do their community building and their affirmations of the life change through affectation. It's overkill.

We see this clearly as outsiders and rightly blame the charlatan leaders for taking advantage of their gullible followers who potentially need psychological help. But we also wrongly assume that the overhauling of a personality in a spiritual context is always, or even mostly, produced by crisis and/or outside agency. By falling under the spell of peer pressure, or a charismatic leader, or maybe even having a good old fashioned midlife crisis. A change in identity has to come from somewhere, we think. And we're right. And we may have correctly identified the problem as originating in one of the above.

But sometimes? Well, sometimes the overwhelming urge to overhaul everything in one's life comes from the universe trying to repackage a person who has experienced the limitless into another set of limitations. If you'll indulge me the time you'd give a caricature artist, I feel I must share with you how I escaped from becoming *that* friend. Adjust you neck pillow. Here we go....

When I was in my late 20s I moved from Westernized, separative, brain-self to all-inclusive heart-self in one transformative moment of understanding. Arriving at the understanding took a few months—or a lifetime, depending on where you start counting. What I newly understood was how I don't actually live an independent existence with problems specific to me. I am an expression of humanity. My problems are not my own; we all share the same problems and we give them to our children. We are, all of us, one stream of consciousness expressing through as many bodies as we create. And the majority of us are polluted with the delusion of separation.

This life-altering flash came as a result of a process of stripping away the layers of me I erroneous called "my psychological baggage," until there was barely anyone left to strip away. Erroneous because that baggage was me, not something different from me that I carried. We would never look down at our hands dangling by our sides and assume they aren't a part of the body just because there is some space between torso and arms. No, they're still part of the body. Still *us*.

Why do we know that about the physical and not the mental, especially given that we talk about them both as possessions?

We say "my hands" and know that we mean as part of "my body." But when we say "my psychological baggage," we mean something like, "my problems, which are not me, but are the concerns I must integrate or recover from so that I may feel better."

When you see yourself as you really are, with 100% clarity, the result is a massive and deeply-uprooting epiphany that properly and healthily contextualizes you. No longer are you divorced from everyone else, from Nature, and from life, this moping, depressed, angry, narcissistic sorrow creature with "my problems." You are now an interconnecting being in the web of life who understands that there is no me with my problems— everyone has problems. We're born into fear and sorrow and we regift them generation to generation. We've done this forever because that's what we do. Until we see it. And then we're out of that cycle.

I had the good fortune of seeing this not intellectually. Not as an idea. Not as something to attain incrementally through self-help books, group therapy, individual therapy, or online motivational blather. I saw it in a flash that changed me as immediately as the word *flash* means. I went from *woe is me* to a person of joy and bliss, acceptance and interconnection, nearly impossible to conceptualize in our society without asking me what drugs I'm on.

The separate sense of self is like a festering blister full of puss, and that is your life. When it pops, you are no longer that puss bubble, obviously. You are, to move past the gross analogy, psychologically healthy and at odds with no one, not even you. You are where you naturally belong. Contented.

Feeling this after having not felt it for as long as you've been alive feels like it must be enlightenment. It isn't. It is correcting the mistakes of a society raised to believe in books. Books that are imaginative human conjurings written to remove us from, and hoist us above, Nature.

"I think therefore I am" is one of our false pedestals. No. *Earth* therefore I am. *Life* therefore I am. *Consciousness in which all life is embedded* therefore I am.

You're getting ahead of myself. Let's go back to how this happened for me and walk up to it together. Perhaps you will discover an epiphany that is not just mine but yours, too. All of ours. Our authentic birthright.

As I wrote in *Urgency.*, I had spent months reading the works of Jiddu Krishnamurti. That's a nice culty guru-sounding name, but he narrowly avoided that trap. From childhood he had been raised to believe that he was the god-man of a Theosophical cult, but was quick to reject the title and the cult in adulthood. This, plus all of the amazing Truth that poured out of his mouth, the likes of which any spiritual cult would have been confused by, made him something of an anti-guru.

Krishnamurti talked about Truth being a pathless land. He spoke of Nothingness as though it was the aliveness in which all is embedded. How there's no path to Nothing because a path is something and Nothing is nothing. All you can do to fruitfully approach the issue is see what he was pointing out so clearly that the brain projecting you stops projecting you. The brain and only the brain can do this because although you may feel like a soul being housed by a body, you're not. You're a function of braincells. A mirage. Sound familiar? I promise I'm not stealing from him, it's just that Truth is Truth. Only the voices speaking it change.

Understanding the above and neither running from it nor embracing it, the spiritual seeker reading the very words of Jiddu Krishnamurti could go silent. Could, that is, *be* Silence, for in the absence of the brain-born self, the self-awareness of Truth becomes that of the body.

Krishnamurti didn't put it exactly like that. He also didn't tell us what happens next. He simply stated words to the effect of, *Understand what I'm saying and find out for yourself.*

And so, as I was reading him, I was employing a tactic on myself that he used often in front of audiences, called *positive negation.* This was where he would proclaim that you cannot say what true Love is, or Beauty, or Joy, et. al.. You cannot say what these big aspects of reality that I capitalize are unless you strip away your everyday concepts of them and attachments to them. Your definitions are your own. Your feelings are your own. If there is a reality to them, perhaps such will reveal itself when you have stripped away all cultural and personal assumptions.

I took Krishnamurti's tool of stripping away the concepts and ideas that keep us from the actual and I used it on myself. I sat alone and examined not the uncapitalized versions of joy and love found in our everyday usage, but my patterns of behavior instead. Why do I behave in the same destructive ways over and over even when I know better? What is my addiction to playing out my weaknesses for?

I followed my breadcrumb trail of remembrances until I found the root causes in my personal history. And then I went further. I looked at why the other people involved, usually my parents, by the end, did what they did. What did I know about their childhoods? How did they learn the same or similar bad patterns of behavior? Further, what did I know about their parents and how they grew up? What about my great-grandparents?

I would scale back as far as I could go in deconstructing my own behavior—which, again, is me. My behavior is me. We like to separate ourselves from our thoughts, our feelings, our behaviors. We put the word "my" in there and think that the ability to phrase it possessively makes them possessions. Try as we might, though, we just can't seem to donate these possessions to charity. That should be our first clue.

I had read enough clues. I was not deconstructing my behavior, I was deconstructing me. And when I came to a resting spot, a plot of land that looked like it held the roots of the problem, I saw that there was land beneath that land. And beneath that land another land. And another. And another. All populated with relatives.

I saw that there was no ending to the fertile soil growing the roots of the problems that comprised me. They went on forever throughout all time in all lives. Not just in my family; everyone shares the same basic root system. Everyone has always shared it. Everyone passes it on. This is what we do. This is humanity.

I am not me. I am not alone. I am not autonomous. That sense of placement in the world is delusional. I am humanity. We appear differentiated on the surface but look deeper and you will find that we share one rootball. No, more than that, we *are* one rootball.

Having deconstructed a number of my psychological motivations, the weight of what it all meant struck me and struck me down. There is no such entity as "Jeremy." The *entity*, as it were, is the human stream of consciousness in a form. Sorrow is all of us.

If that sounds depressing it's because you are a thought construct trying to remain intact and you have to run to the worst plausible interpretation of what I'm writing to do that. I have an easy solution for this: stop reading and deconstruct yourself. Positively negate a few of what you think are your psychological problems. You likely won't have to run down the entire list to come to our basic human core. You just have to look, and look honestly. The act of looking honestly is clarity. Not clarifying—*clarity*. You have never done this before. I know because to do it is to be it. That's the whole point here. And right now? You aren't clarity, you're screwed up. Because that's what you're used to being.

Fortunately for people feeling their mortality, this doesn't take forever. It ain't psychotherapy. You don't have to read volumes of Krishnamurti or anyone else to step out of the stream of sorrow, either. It is one thing to read words and get them conceptually or feel them relationally. It's another thing to be transformed through doing the work on yourself. When that happens you are recontextualized in the snap of a finger. Like a magic trick. The separate-self identity you just were is now an interconnecting identity with not just all of humanity but all life. All existence. It is so new and yet remembered—

so whole and completely real—that it feels like it must be enlightenment.

If you've ever learned anything about what spiritual enlightenment allegedly is, this bliss state of interconnectivity, acceptance, understanding, empathy, and unclenched gentleness must be it. It is beyond euphoric. You literally wake up into a healthier sense of consciousness. It is true freedom and you have immediate compassion for those around you who don't know themselves as you didn't one breath ago. They are you, after all.

What is this state of mind if not enlightenment?

It is health. I call it moving from brain-self to heart-self. More clearly, and perhaps less controversially, it is dissolving the false autonomy of the separate self for natural interconnection. It is the healthy contextualization of you within the web of life. This is not something that, for instance, First Nations peoples who never lost their connection have to go through. It is "enlightenment" for adults who grew up stuck in their heads. Adults from literate cultures. Cultures of religions and science. This enlightenment we feel is the everyday existence of most natural cultures—the ones that didn't overpopulate and form corrupted governments or other damaging hierarchies.

Most people I know have grown up with science dictating how reality should be. With religion dictating how reality should be. Grown up trapped in a society that aspires to selfishness through capitalism. Grown up, that is, in a complex of contradictory systems and beliefs that stunt our growth.

Because we're used to our limitations, we call our struggle *human nature*. By and large, struggling is what humans do and yet our friction and sorrow are unhealthy. Creating an inner world of delusion and spreading that outwardly is unnatural and unhealthy, even though it's inevitable.

Western psychology tells us that the healthiest among us are mildly delusional. The least health are psychotic. Again, this spectrum is accurate enough, but the spectrum does not have to be our mind. This is the spectrum of human consciousness as we live it the further and further away we drift from our natural sense of self as a single being embedded within, and interconnecting with, all.

Although Krishnamurti never explicitly stated that this move to heart is what happens, it is inevitable. It's the inevitable outcome of understanding ourselves, which is why he refused to tantalize us with it. Giving us a goal would keep us from it. Keep us stuck in the head looking for heart. Keep us from a transformation that is, again, not a normal epiphany through knowledge. Not a come-and-go feeling. Not a supposition or a wish of a fatigued, delusional mind repeating a mantra. It's a big ol' proverbial lightbulb going off the size of the likely still proverbial sun. A new normal actualized through instantaneous transformation.

And I thought this was it. I thought this was enlightenment. I was being flooded with wisdom from the ether in the way that, mere moments ago, I had average thoughts coming to me. Sex and movie quotes, mostly. Now, those thoughts were good, joyful, disciplined, relaxing yet passionately felt feelings that birthed through me as words of wisdom. They were words I was living as that, when spoken, became words to live by for the untransformed listener. They were complete thoughts. Unerringly correct. They were Truth whispering through me.

Uttering such powerful words, unfortunately, is how religions start. It's how wise men and women gain legendary status as sages. These words are Truth speaking Oneself through your and my body. In my case, through this Jeremy character now conscious of the fact that he was a character being projected by the body. That he was timeless awareness flowing into time as thought. Thought, which I still was. I was both.

I was a thought construct, but now there was also Truth thinking me. I was recontextualized into heart. Was no longer trapped in rationalizations and the delusion that I would come to clarity through the fog of thinking. I knew myself as a mind within a system of mind within a system of other minds, and Truth, which transcends and includes all of us. Truth, now as a friend, as a mentor, speaking through me because, even though I knew Truth was me, wisdom still came as if *to* me, not exactly *as* me. Mine was a 2nd-person experience of Truth, not 1st-person as Truth.

***

All along our lives divisions in the oneness that we are want to weed their way in. But I hadn't realized this then —at least not about me—because with division comes ego inflation. This was mine: I fooled myself into believing that because I was he who was aware of his conniving mind, I was impervious to experiencing divisions. Truth was a pathless land and I assumed I had teleported to this land.

I mean, really: how could this not be the big enlightenment of myth and lore? What else could it possibly be?

Well, as great and revolutionary as this state was, it wasn't it. Yes, this was healthy in a way radically different than how I was a moment ago, but this wasn't extra. This wasn't beyond me. This wasn't the death of me. This was me in relief of a false identity. I realized it one random day while I was sitting on my couch in my apartment in Manhattan's East Village—ever a spiritual location if there was one—reading (who else?) Jiddu Krishnamurti. As my eyes took in his words, my mind momentarily fluttered with the realization that, 'Wait! Krishnamurti isn't just talking about the release of a separate-self identity into this web-of-life identity, he's talking about the complete cessation of self! And we will do anything to avoid that because that's death. I, in my avoidance of death, mistook the recontextualization of self as the death of self. I still have an identity. I'm now *that* guy. The guy who reads Krishnamurti and spouts off words of wisdom. I'm the guy who completely gets Krishnamurti. I could probably teach him if I wanted to. I have the wisdom coming to me. *I'm. That. Guy.*'

In moving to heart I had cleverly dropped one identity for another. This realization performed a magic trick: it killed me. Finished me off. My sense of self didn't wake up to another even better-feeling version of me, I vanished totally. In my wake Nothing was the case. And that's indescribable because it is neither conscious nor unconscious. It's literally nothing.

And then... then something.

Then I'm back. Jer 2.0, as I've jokingly called it. Nothing gives way to a thing: awareness. Silence gives way to sound: the sound of me aware. I am alive. And I am not alone.

With me is this massive Secret of Silence: the Intelligence of Silence in the form of action. Not just wisdom, but that, too. Now, also, a willpower charging up the backside and into the head. An energy moving the body around as if by a second will. A now ever-present revolutionary energy. An energy that moves the body into yogic postures, mudras, Dervish twirls, exercises that look like Tai Chi, that look like acupressure, that look like regular stretches, that look like a host of coordinated movements I don't do on my own and don't know anything about beyond everyday stretches.

That's some of it.

When the Intelligence of Silence acts I am not acting. If I try to anticipate a move I get in the way and am more often wrong than not, similar to scaling Pololū Valley barefooted. So me on my best behavior is me witnessing this as it's happening, not me trying to help.

I don't go anywhere. I'm not in a disassociated state. I'm not hypnotized. I'm not detached, hovering above the body watching. You may talk to me as this other will is performing. And when I reassert myself, the other will stops. I am a glorified on/off switch to a willpower much healthier for the body than I ever was.

***

The Will of Silence began with small movements: my head circling around, my right hand gesticulating, these sorts of things that would just happen on their own, and I could either let them go on or stop them. But it also began with some pain, for, if you'll recall, in that initial moment of me dying and resurrecting with this new energy surging, two disks herniated in my back. It seemed a minor physical issue that I assumed would correct itself in a few days.

Weeks.

Months.

It never did because, truth be told, I was a moron. I ignored an issue that plainly required medical attention and made it worse over a span of months to the extent that I finally became immobile and couldn't work. In that immobilization I wound up in Mt. Sinai Hospital on morphine. The emergency room doctor told me I needed back surgery. He quickly corrected himself, however, when he found out I didn't have health insurance. Then the medical solution became that I needed to leave the hospital as soon as I could hobble out of there. Hilariously, someone on the staff gave me the number to a physical therapist who wouldn't even take my call. No insurance.

I won't say this was all a blessing in disguise but I will tell you that it resulted in me lying in bed with no other choice but to take a chance and let this Will of Silence—this meditation energy, as I took to calling it—move freely. What did I have to lose? Heck, what else did I even have to do?

Ultimately, the secondary will power got me into decent enough shape that I could go back to work and finally afford el cheapo physical therapy. Turns out that riding a stationary bike and being administered ultrasound therapy week in and week out are no match for the healing maneuverings of the Will of Silence. In my case, the best physical therapy was free.

After I recovered physically (my spine was never 100% after that, but 90% will do) I let the energy do its thing regularly. I stayed out of the way and watched it unfold in a process of not just physical betterment but also psychic awakenings. I had anticipated none of this. I had expected none of this. I was flabbergasted by all of it and hugely interested. I couldn't wait to see what would happen next or if it would stop. It felt like I was being given tastes of psychic experiences so that I would have clarity about them.

Dormant psychic centers I didn't believe in were being dusted off and activated within me regardless of my skepticism, but I wasn't interested in honing any of the new abilities that came with them. Because of my nonattached attitude I was running the gamut of them, being shown their reality and their limitations so I could have real discernment about them, not just blind acceptance or rejection of other people's claims.

Whatever I was becoming didn't go unnoticed by the universe at large. Shortly after coming clear with wisdom from the Intelligence of Silence, and then coming alive with the Will of Silence, I received a response of sorts from the universe. It was essentially a response from form and time to my having "adopted" formless, timeless Intelligence. It was the response of wanting to convert that which transcends and includes the universe to something that exists within the universe, no different than when people want to hoard enlightenment experiences for their personal growth, but on a slightly grander scale. You know: *universal*.

Normally people want to be the ones in control of enlightenment. They don't want to die for enlightenment to be the case. Of course not. They want to have an experience that is theirs. Theirs to brag about. Or teach. Or feel loved by. We are the universe and the universe is just as controlling as we are. Arguably, the reason we are so is because we're behaving as the universe needs us to in order to grow.

The only way the universe grows is by attaining novel experiences from outside itself—in this case from Truth coming through a body. We experience this outside-in force as inside-out. It comes through us, as us, out into the world. This is what humans are on our best day. We are Truth flowing through a body. And the universe loves it when we have best days, it just doesn't want us to live our best lives. Truth coming through us is acceptable. Truth as us is not.

Sad to say, the universe doesn't want Truth to be our 1st-person identity. It wants us to treat Truth like an extraordinary state of mind that we visit and come back from because living as Truth is the death of body-self identity. And our bodies are nothing if not comprised of the universe. Not just existing in some vessel called *the universe*. We *are* that. We are matter. Solidified energy. One fabric, different hues. The universe wants us to have experiences that we share and reinforce and build structures out of. This is exactly the same as saying the universe itself wants to have those experiences itself.

Now, when a lucky person like me wins the lottery of understanding so thoroughly that I dissolve and Truth becomes me, the universe's reflexive reaction is to try like hell to contextualize me. It does this by landing *Jeremy 2.0* within a different archetype than whatever I was unconsciously living in before. It wants me to be a bohemian.

Okay, maybe not exactly that in my case, but…. Here. Let me show you what I do mean exactly. In *Urgency*. I talked about Jiddu Krishnamurti for the same obvious reason I introduced him here: reading him and getting him, I became him.

No, just kidding. Reading him and getting him, I died and the Will of Silence came alive in the body. I came alive again, too. And I did not become Krishnamurti. I didn't even want to. Believe it or not, that's the strange part, as we'll see in a bit, and that's why we need to stick with him now. What we're about to discover together is so important, no one has even talked about it until I opened my yapper. If they have, show it to me. I could be wrong. You've got thousands of years of literature on your side, show me where it is. I mean that arrogantly, but not as arrogantly as it sounds. I'd really like to know if this has been explicitly stated anywhere.

What is it?

It is this....

Jiddu Krishnamurti was born in India, schooled in the United Kingdom, and resided in North America until his death in 1986. None of these countries are China. None of these countries are Japan. And yet, as I was going through the awakening, even though this Indian boy turned Western anti-guru adult was my only real influence, I felt a strong pull to adopt a cartoonish hodgepodge of cultural traits from China and Japan.

Really, the pull was toward assimilating what I perceived to be from ancient Chinese culture: Buddhist stuff, contemplative stuff, discipline stuff, ancient stuff, movie stuff, TV stuff, the stuff of Hollywood and maybe History Channel. But that compulsion to assume new customs and ways of being in the world that fit my identity, as you can tell from my superficial list of influences and lack of education, was my ignorance talking. And talking loudly, because when it came to my fashion sensibilities, I wanted desperately to abandon my frumpy whatever-was-in-my-closet wardrobe for the silk kimonos I gawked at longingly every time I strolled by the shop window of the Kimono House in SoHo where they hung, enticingly. Expensively.

Oh, but wait. Kimonos are Japanese, not Chinese. I didn't know that at the time. Or care. I just wanted to dress Chinese. And that's only one example of the ignorant change I wanted to inflict upon myself to merge with the Americanized vision of an archetypal spiritual-but-not-religious Eastern otherworldliness. Don't get me started on what I wanted to do with my hair.

If I was your average weak-willed youngster being influenced by some spiritual teacher to adopt his shtick, I'd be doing it up Krishnamurti-style. I'd be emulating an Indian man with ties to Britain and America. An Indian man who wore neatly pressed collared shirts and neckties. Slacks and belts. Loafers, probably, I don't remember. He dressed like a White middle management guy, not someone out of *Shogun*.

Wait, what did they wear in *Shogun*? I don't remember that either. The ignorance is real, folks. The ignorance is real.

And yet, as these authentic spiritual awakenings were amping up and unfolding and different parts of me were coming online, coming alive, changing my sense of identity, transitioning me from normal Jeremy to Jeremy plus Truth to just Truth with Jeremy as an afterthought, there was this pushback by the universe itself to make me someone who fit the clichéd profile of "enlightenment seeker," or more confidently and worse, "enlightened guru." It was a push to shovel my flowering state of timeless being into a prepackaged identity with some new interests back in good ol' time.

If the universe had its way I would have stepped into a different archetypal pattern of behavior with all the time-filler games of meditating, engaging weak psychic abilities, and following synchronicities and gut feelings on a personal growth journey that would have left me none the wiser. No doubt I would have worked hard to spread that story, complete with demonstrations of my power, to an eager audience.

Yes, the universe tried to dumb me down with an absurd shallow exterior to hide the depths, which is weird because I do a pretty good job of that on my own. Mercifully for me and everyone who knew me and would have been embarrassed for me, one of the beauties of understanding Krishnamurti is being able to avoid falling into the trap of coalescing a self-identity around any new unfolding trait, such as psychic awakenings. Sure, when the Intelligence of Silence activated visions in me, I could have stopped there. I could have concentrated on them, explored them, learned to turn them on and off, perhaps mastered them, and sold expensive remote viewing workshops so that you too could be a master of seeing stuff in your head, just like me. But even as the psychic awakenings were happening I knew that becoming their exponent and salesman would be a mistake.

For some reason, though, it was harder for me to see through the ploy of drawing me to Asian cultures. Not much harder, but a bit. I'm certain if I'd had the money I would have bought at least one silk kimono and walked around town looking like a jackass and feeling great about myself. I wouldn't have cared what anyone thought about it.

Eventually, I would have degraded into some mutant form of pretentious hipster listening to record albums and sipping Starbucks French Roast from a mason jar. I would have been culturally appropriating from the wrong culture and, little doubt, would be an incel to this day. But, man alive, I'd have owned Neutral Milk Hotel's *In the Aeroplane Over the Sea* on vinyl and that's all that would have mattered. Not to listen to, mind you, because in my wholeness I no longer needed music, but to display amongst my Happy Buddha statue, tabletop waterfall, and handmade Tai Chi sword I inevitably would have saved up for.

I mean, right?

One digresses....

I had a sneaky suspicion that because I was approaching all of this in an honest and clear way, I wasn't succumbing to ego inflation. Looking back now, I further see that because I was going through this process in the right way, the universe had to act fast by pressuring me to adopt a new identity or lose me to Truth forever. What was the point of the universe allowing me to acquire what it sees as Truth's building blocks for itself if it wasn't going to be able to use me to build anything with them?

I was no longer Jeremy the sarcastic dude who just wanted to write and direct for film and TV and make comedies for a living. Before you say it, yes I am still sarcastic, obviously. But I'm not attached to it. Real non-attachment isn't about rejecting or accepting who you are. The me of attachments sloughed off naturally like old skin. The objects of attachment still existed in my life, I just had no desire for or against them.

Alarmed by this, the universe went into overdrive trying to replace my old skin. Replace me. Because the universe at large recognized that I had been shed.

If I may describe it a bit mechanically here, I had been living as one cluster of repeating behaviors in an archetype that was no longer pertinent when I became Nothing. Because the universe is all things, it must reject Nothing. It cannot afford for me to be Nothing. The death of me in this way is the death of the universe—or at least a major wound inflicted upon it. Thus, it needed me to be something. To be someone. To adopt a new behavior cluster within a different archetype. The end result of this archetypal shell game is that I would remain a body-derived self of psychological time in the universe.

I need to say this again without repeating it boringly because I suspect it's hard to absorb. The universe is time, is things. And so it wants you to remain a thing of time. It doesn't want you to shed thingness and time for Nothingness. The way the universe grows is through new experiences. It may cast people into nonduality now and then like tackle on a fishing line, or allow people to have transcendental experiences, so as to incorporate the newness of nondual being within itself as experiences. Once captured, nonduality breaks into dualities—into visions, visionary journeys, the land of the dead, DMT trips, plant medicine journeys, hierarchical states and stages of consciousness with godheads and otherworldly intelligences. Into, that is, the formless underbelly of the physical universe. These and more are carnival ride virtual versions of the real. Yes, even totally serious Buddhist meditations bring you to the cosmic amusement park, which is why the universe was fine and dandy with me identifying with whatever dumb notion I had of Buddhists.

How can I know? How can I tell?

The difference between the real and the carbon copy is fundamentally this: the real is you, always. It is the first-person identity *as* you when the body stops projecting its version of the thing called "you."

The virtual is not you. It is you having an experience. And that experience may be gotten to through repetitions such as prayer, repentance, meditation, breath work, yoga. mantras, creative visualizations, and so on. All of the ways in which we claim to practice spirituality will, when done in earnest, eventually bring you to their prophesied self-fulfillment.

In Truth, spirituality has no practice and no destination to work toward. But in the carnival of human mind, maybe you'll have a conversation with "God." Or be in union with "Goddess." And it will feel real. It may actually *be* real in the sense that those gods could be other sentient thought forms just like you and me.

You will reach that higher spiritual vibration, that new density, that further rung on the ladder of personal evolution. Of course you will if you concentrate hard enough. The universe needs these hierarchies, needs these states and stages of consciousness, because they are its interiority. Its interiority provides the options for your interiority, and you cannot sustain yourself forever in the liminal state of trying. You have to eventually achieve something.

States and stages of consciousness are expressed through you. What you achieve is a new illusion of movement and a different coat of paint. Meanwhile, it's all you. And, Truth be told, it's also already written. That is to say, whatever you feel you're deciding to do next has already been done, you just don't know that you've experienced it yet.

None of this, by the way, is a trap or evil or some form of awful hell. The universe is not secretly the devil trying to oppress you or trap you in time. It's just the duck egg you were born as and into. To differentiate from the shell is to crack open and waddle away. Same principle here.

If this all sounds like a silly stretch of the imagination, look no further than yourself for an analogous scenario. Truth is not an illness or an injury, but as comparisons go it's in the same ballpark. How much of your youth was spent throwing yourself into situations that begot illness or injury? And why? Because your body needed to internalize the external to learn from it. Namely, to learn how to fend off illness and injury. The body does that—you do that—to build much-needed strengths like knowledge, reflexes, antibodies, and personal boundaries, which not only act as resistances but add onto you with things like new viruses, new antibodies, psychological maturity, discipline, and the knowledge of what not to do. Like, don't eat candy found in a mud puddle, you'll get sick. Knowledge like that.

Look, you are this whether you know it or not. To say that the universe is confining you is to say that you are doing it to yourself. You are doing it to yourself unconsciously until you understand all of this. The understanding comes equipped with its own discipline. It's kind of like how there are people who have pitch-perfect hearing. They understand when even the tiniest hidden note in a song is off key. The rest of us can't pick up on the sour note because we don't have that perfect hearing. That's the type of ear, as it were, that I and people like me have for reality.

However, we can ignore it. And we can be enticed away from it. The second we do that, it's like Dorothy veering off the path to Oz—she's asleep in the poppy fields again. Back to psychological time we go.

Maintaining our pitch perfect hearing involves neither accepting nor rejecting any of the notes: perfect, slightly off, way off—it doesn't matter. Just sticking with what is happening now matters. Whatever is playing is what's playing. We're not accepting or rejecting because we're not the one playing it. Attachment is no longer our song and so the unfolding process is allowed to play out without us getting in the way with all of our big dumb ideas. Not even to learn about it.

Back to me as an example, when I entered a period of psychic experiences that lasted a few months, first up were auditory hallucinations, for lack of a better term, then visual. I could have stuck with either of them and said, "Oh, wow. I'm a psychic. I need to develop these abilities now." But that would be me losing my pitch perfect hearing and going out of tune.

Temptation is there all along the way to become something because the universe is perpetually tempting you—which is the same as saying that you are tempting yourself—back to self-centeredness. Both are the same. It's you all the way down. And when you know this by having worked through yourself, the call to become someone great is just background static. There's no real power in those temptations for power.

Not initially, anyway. But give it a couple of years. A couple of years after you've deconstructed your personal psychology and moved to heart. After you've further dissolved to Nothing and then reformed as Me 2.0. The fact that you cannot be the old psychological issues you once were doesn't stop them from tugging on you like hungry ghosts. They want to be you again even though they can never be you again. They're everlastingly nagging you and they grow louder with the years. It's as if your brain has the patterns of old behaviors forever etched into it, but like a matrix of dry river beds, there's no water left to run through them and give them life.

This is a common issue for people who think they are enlightened. It is why integral psychologist Ken Wilber claims that it is possible for, oh, name your favorite fallen guru, to be a spiritual 10 and a psychological 2. He notes that you may wake up through transcendental experiences, but you also need to grow up, psychologically. Preferable first. And most allegedly enlightened people think that by waking up they *have* grown up.

Cue starting a sex cult.

That's the way Wilber justifies the discrepancy between simultaneous psychological lows and spiritual highs in a person. And I would respond with a reminder that all of this waking and growing business takes place along a manmade hierarchy within the confines of the universe. It's just a nice, clever way to keep such a one trapped here, perpetually working on themselves.

The waking/growing split becomes an issue only when you deny your pitch perfect hearing. Although such a one may continue to speak Truth indirectly, that one ain't Truth speaking directly. Glossing over the distinction between being Truth speaking and being you again speaking truths is the trigger for living an unconscious, delusional life. Again. But, you know, a higher one. *Delusional Me 2.0: A Higher Me With Ghosts.*

Fallen angel though you may be, you can never go home again to those old transparent patterns. But you sure can make new opaque ones! Worse ones. Because you haven't grown up enough to come to terms with all of this. This is the point at which Wilber is correct. I stress, it's only if you fall.

But, like, you probably will fall. So, he's more right than I'm giving him credit for.

I suppose it's not much different than a famous musician who falls from the spotlight and spends the rest of his or her life chasing fame again with the especially delusional mindset that they are not chasing it because they never lost it. They're just one smash hit away from capturing the old glory, you'll see. You'll all see.

Meanwhile, there is no falling. No ascending. Just everyone dancing on the ceiling.

Ask Lionel Richie. He was the Mary Poppins of 1986.

Chapter 14
Cuddle Fish III:
Breakin' All The Fishy Rules

Say, whatever did happen to me in my New York heyday of growing up a little and waking up a lot? How did I avoid becoming a kimono hipster douchebag? What's the secret there?

Glad you asked. I veer offtrack sometimes. I did warn you to adjust your neck pillow.

It really was our good friend poverty that kept me from becoming a culturally-appropriating master within the Archetype of Clichés. Is that a thing? Subgenre: Spiritually Awakened White Guy. That *is* a thing, right?

Spiritually Awakened White Guy wanted to be Asian all of a sudden, wanted to grow his hair long and put it in a ponytail, wanted to dress the part, wear the loose clothing, do the yoga, do the martial arts to some extent, or, you know, I was still a fat guy—let's not go too far. These were not just personal fantasies of what I felt drawn to become. They were fantasies being reinforced by the universe as the correct direction I needed to steer my life.

How did the universe attempt to achieve this, you ask? Ah. Another excellent question, Grasshopper. The universe spoke to me through synchronicities and high strangeness experiences.

For example, I went through a period of having visions flicker into 3-D life behind my eyelids whenever my head would hit the pillow. Not fall asleep, mind you, but literally when I would lie down and shut my eyes, there were people waiting for me. Indian and Chinese, I thought. I inherently knew them to be Buddhas even though I had only the slightest comprehension of what that meant. I would see them; they would see me. They'd be smiling in an unspoken acknowledgment like, "Hey, welcome to the club. Enlightenment's kinda cool, right?"

This led to a number of nights in a row where I dreamt of being shown around different parts of a recurring location by Asian people I assumed were Chinese. As I described in *Urgency.*, this dream location was like a dojo in hell, but not hell the way Christians think of hell. Some other version that's much milder. I don't remember if I considered it hell because of an innate feeling or something communicated to me, but it probably had to do with the giant portrait of a demon on the wall whom I knew ran the place. I don't know how I knew that, I just did. And yet what was this place? It was primarily a yoga dojo where people were stretching on mats beneath the demon wall hanging. Not too hellish by Dante's standards.

My same Asian hosts showed me around other floors of this building in different dreams, but I don't remember much about them. Nothing as drastic as that one. What I remember most was the Will of Silence moving my hands around in these dreams similar to the way it makes them gesticulate in real life. I knew, or felt like I knew, that what it was doing was both sustaining my form in this realm and protecting me from potential attack. By what, I don't know. How's all that work? Don't know.

To be completely transparent, I am not certain that's what the hand movements were about, but it had the feeling of, like, I'm in another realm and these mudras inoculate me and keep me equalized so that I may traverse the depths of the underworld for as long as my hosts need to show me around different levels of this building.

Some weeks after the recurring dreams died down I was paid a surprise visit in the waking world from the dream demon. I will forgive you for not believing me, but disbelief won't change the fact that the demon from the portrait actually inhabited this here body for maybe 15 seconds in waking life. He savored the taste of physical living in this dimension through me and then left.

And then there was this one time when I self-identified as the universe exploding into existence from Nothing, and Spirit soaring through the vast expanse like the ultimate thrill ride.

Enough, already, am I right? Wisdom is easy to digest. You'd think the paranormal events encasing wisdom would be capsules that wash down just as smoothly. Nope. They are dry, rocky shucks that our society cracks open and discards as myth or allegory. They, like wisdom, are experiential. And they don't just occur internally.

What was occurring with moi outside—way outside on the streets of New York—that is worth writing about here was a sophisticated series of quiet protests by Falun Gong practitioners. Falun Gong is a cult that sprouted up in Changchun, Jilin Province of China in 1992. It takes from Buddhism and Taoism, like s'mores take from chocolate and marshmallow, and focuses heavily on qigong practice. At least that's what I read online just now to sound smart as I type this. Not the s'mores part; that was my contribution.

Oh, also, they are banned in China because *reasons*. That part I knew. So they're a cult that does yoga and meditation and that sort of thing, essentially.

Because Falun Gong was banned in China, its practitioners were raising awareness of their persecution and torture by setting up little scenes on sidewalks around Manhattan that illustrated their plight. Scenes like a practitioner being held in a makeshift jail cell where a guard with a baton would beat the crap out of him. The people acting in the scene would have to hold their action stances all day long like statues while a representative handed out leaflets. Perhaps this was a ploy to get the public interested in Falun Gong practice, because we'd be left wondering how they can be so disciplined as to hold a pose all day long in the middle of the bustling city. How did they develop the superpowers of a mime without mime school? Where do we sign up?

The intrigue of their motionless performance art was likely as much a draw as trying to figure out why they were there in the first place. God knows no one was going to read the leaflet. At least I wasn't—and I stopped to watch these displays around town more than a few times. Had plenty of leaflets. Plenty of time to read.

A funny thing started happening when I stopped to take in the scenes at different locations with different protestors doing the freeze-frame mime work. It happened twice, both times during my building obsession with Asian cultures that I knew nothing about and was too poor to engage with in any wardrobe-altering way. Twice, the people whose entire job was to not move a muscle all day long subtly turned to me, nodded their heads, and then turned back. The cop did it in one scene and someone else did it in another. I don't remember what the second person's role was, or what the scene was, for that matter, but you never forget your first. I remember the cop because the man playing the role had on a police hat, aviator shades—the whole getup. It was like being in a scene from a fantasy movie where the unwitting, reluctant hero (that's right, *me*) is being acknowledged by a secret society who knows what I don't: I'm one of them.

This made quite the impression on me. When I subsequently happened upon these scenes, I made it a habit to watch at a slight distance to see if any of the actors broke and nodded at other random people. They did not. It was obvious to me that these people I'd never met were singling me out. Kind of a creepy but cool mystery that I was okay letting hang like that.

Oh, but it didn't end there.

This Asian cinema secret society I was Main Character Syndroming in—I mean starring in—had a third act. I was waiting for the train in an underground subway station. This little old Asian lady hunching over a cart rolled up behind me and tapped me on the back. I turned around and looked down. She was tiny. I don't think she knew English. She just kind of grunted at me and pushed a newspaper into my delicate, barely-worked, White privileged hands. At this point in my life I'd had enough experience with synchronicities to know that this was something odd, something to pay attention to. Just to be sure, I monitored her as she left. She didn't bug anyone else, didn't hand out newspapers to another soul down there. She gave the paper to me and then rolled her cart up to the stairs and slowly rolled her old bag of bones on out of there, one begrimed concrete step at a time, mission accomplished.

I was her mission. She came there just to give me a paper. Perhaps her entire life had led to this moment. In the movie version that's exactly what happened. She either somehow recognized me as part of the same invisible college she was in or something in her compelled her to approach me. I know this sounds like self-aggrandizement. And it was. But not from me. I was just noticing this. The universe was trying to aggrandize me. Trying to rope me into some Asian subculture by making me feel special.

But why?

I looked at the headline of the newspaper the woman had practically forced on me. The top story was about Falun Gong being repressed in China. 'Ah,' I thought. 'There it is again.'

Now, why did she not hand papers to any other White guy? Or Asian guy? Or any other guy? I mean, no one? No women? Nobody? Children don't read? Just me?

Weird, right?

Months later I found the answer to why me when I visited my sister at Yale University. She was attending grad school there, and in this scene of my biopic I was browsing through the Yale bookstore when I just happened to stumble upon a small hardcover written by political science professor Maria Hsai Chang, titled, *Falun Gong: The End of Days*. It was about the origins of Falun Gong, their beliefs, their fast rise in popularity, and the Chinese government's concern and response. I leafed through until my synchronistically-tuned fingers stopped on the right page. The page the universe, if not the university, wanted me to find. There, I read that the leader of Falun Gong, Li Hongzhi, believed he was receiving channeled messages from moon men. That's right, aliens living on the moon. It's more than that, but it is basically that. Falun Gong whittles down to allegedly channeled alien info. That's what the cult is. Their qigong movements, their poses, all of it comes from aliens.

Aliens. I was no stranger to aliens, having been a witness to several UFOs over the course of my life and an experiencer of what I used to think were alien abductions.

Years spent rubbing my chin astutely as I pondered my own odd life brought me to realize that I didn't honestly know what the phenomenon was, but *alien abduction* was a social construct that was too limiting to describe the events and their effects.

At any rate, the topic had been of obsessive importance to me since 8th grade. How perfect this Falun Gong discovery was. A little too perfect for my taste. As if some hidden hand was guiding me to transfer all of what was happening to me with the spiritual stuff and the wholeness stuff onto my passion and my, really, partial self-identity in the world of alien abductions.

This on-the-nose temptation to hitch my wagon to Falun Gong was its own deal killer. It was one step too far for me. I was just fine browsing large flea markets on weekends for the inevitable table of Buddhist statuettes I could examine for familiar poses and facial expressions. I would stare at them and try to decipher their meaning, what they were for, because the Will of Silence often positioned my body in those same ancient ways, including my face. Finding little clues and studying them was enough for me. I didn't need the hassle of exploring some ridiculous Chinese alien yoga cult.

That said, I would have looked amazing in a kimono. You know it. I know it.

Japanese! Kimonos are Japanese! And I was still associating all of this spirit stuff with Chinese spirituality, which I shouldn't have. Not wholly, anyway, because some of the people in my visions were not Chinese. Nobody enlightened was White, naturally, but there were a couple of men farting around in my head whom I took to be Indian. And the Will of Silence didn't only do yoga movements and Buddha-statue hand gestures. It performed cross-cultural movements from around the globe. Muslim-themed prostrations and Sufi Whirling Dervish twirls spring to mind. And there's that one time, soon after moving to Hawaii, when I decided to let the Will of Silence speak the body. This was on December 21, 2012, the end of the Mayan calendar's 13-baktun cycle. Also the end of the world, except that part was a wee bit overstated. What happened instead, to this body, anyway, was... wait for it... a hula dance.

As I look at all of this now, what I see is that the universe was trying to coax me into adopting an identity so that I could live in a new normal as the type of douchebag only a special few ever really get the glory of becoming. Thankfully, or perhaps regrettably (kimonos, damn it, kimonos), I didn't end up that douchebag. I ended up *this* douchebag.

I'm grateful the universe gave up on me. But I'm also glad to have participated in the revelation of one of the secrets of, well, noise. It's one of the secrets of the spiritual seeker and of the universe: the universe is, in a sense, a thought construct. And the human self is, in every sense, a thought construct. It's only natural for the universe in which we are embedded to want us to adopt a persona and stay there for as long as possible.

If you ever get the inkling that your life needs a complete spiritual overhaul, the universe would like you to interpret that as, *Oh, I don't need an instantaneous transformation through the death of me, which is the death of time. I need self-evolution through time. I need to evolve through learning.* And with that evolution, that growth, you will switch archetypes. You will develop a zest for new patterns of behavior that, like all patterns, are predetermined.

Yes, if the universe has its way, you're going to switch associations from who you are now to the next best you.

But any switch you make is still within you. You still exist, experiencing a facsimile of transformation, a facsimile of the new. It's new to you. New enough, right? Tickling the belly butterflies and all that? Triggering the nervous system in a good way for a hot minute?

Then the echo of repressed Truth surfaces just enough for you to feel your partiality and you grow restless and bored and move to the next "new" fascination. Surely *that* will complete you.

This is the weight on our spiritual barbell, folks. And I don't know that anyone has spoken about this until right now in this way. Maybe Welsh Harlequin—*Croak! Croak!*—but good luck figuring him out.

***

Now let's talk fish and talk recap. Talk about how the universe pushing back to retain you by redefining you is a defense mechanism much the same as the cuttlefish's shapeshifting, only the universe's camouflage for us is archetypal. That archetype, if you're not careful, becomes the new you. The new you looks suspiciously like an old version of someone else. A lot of someone elses. A cliché. You become a cliché if you step into the role given you.

Silence has a secret discipline. So too does the universe that wants you back. And so you now have to be alert enough to tell the difference between authentic communication from nondual beings, an oxymoron we have yet to deeply explore, sorry to spring it on you, and the universe faking it to subsume you back within itself via a context or archetype. The difference is subtle and it requires pitch-perfect hearing, which we don't have. We are out of tune. Thus, when we listen to Silence we hear numerous voices. We hear ourselves first. This is why prisoners locked in solitary confinement tend to go insane. The last person you wholly want to be with is you, or else you'd never relegate your taboo desires and behaviors to the unconscious basement of selfhood.

Only Silence hears Silence as it is. One Silence. One consciousness. One ceiling. Our divisions are not real. However, we live as though they are, therefore they are. They are until they aren't.

Then, like the cuttlefish.... *Tilt!*

Chapter 15
Sanctuary

Whenever Carol or I tell people we raise ducks they give us the smirk of having received a quirky surprise. Why ducks and not chickens? Chickens are everywhere on the island—you could practically trip over a hen and throw her in the back of the truck. Heck, why not other farm animals like goats or sheep while we're at it?

Well, we did our homework on chickens vs. ducks. Ducks are much easier to round up at night and less likely to wander off during the day, never to be seen again. Ducks need their watering hole after all. Also, Carol liked that ducks don't have claws and sharp beaks, which could spell disaster if they ever got fed up with us.

As for other animals, we toyed with the idea, but they're a lot of work and require fencing all around the land. We didn't want to imprison ourselves like that, nor could we afford to. No, birds made the best sense, especially given that we considered our home a bird sanctuary.

The reality of this being a sanctuary hit us shortly after we moved here in 2016, what with all the carefully-planned tree lines planted in the middle of dry pastureland. We felt like it was our duty to maintain this oasis because everyone needs a respite, especially the plovers who fly in from Alaska every winter, and sight-seeing Volcano birds.

Volcano is the artfully named general vicinity on and around Hawaii's most active volcano, Kilauea. There's Hawaii Volcanoes National Park and Volcano Village. Doesn't matter what comes before or after the word *volcano*, it is all condensed to just *Volcano* in the local parlance. And every living being, every parcel of ground, even the air and the light and the shadows there, have a distinct edge to them. It's as if normal Hawaii isn't awe-inspiring enough, Volcano exists in 16K with the contrast maxed out. This is equally true for birdsongs, which are sung with sharply delineated notes.

Carol and I started hearing some of those Volcano birdsongs at our home many months after we settled in and realized that different birds migrate here during different seasons, including snowbirds, which are monied old people—but we don't give them sanctuary. Knowing this, we were really excited for our place to be a vacation spot for birds. And now, thanks in part to the Will of Silence, this bird oasis comes equipped with a mobile hospital.

A mobile hospital?

A mobile hospital. *Me.*

Naturally, I have a long-winded story for this....

One sunny day months ago I woke up earlier than usual and got to work editing essays for my website, OurUndoing.com, when I heard the smack of a bird crashing into the kitchen window. Bird crashes were not a common occurrence, but they happened now and then. To my mind it was odd that birds crashed here at all because our windows had curtains that were almost always closed. In fact the one bare window we did have? No birds smashed into it. Ever. They all seemed to want to dart into the windows that had curtains.

I don't know what that's about, but most of the time it's not terribly traumatic for the winged people. Most of the time the unlucky bird smacks into a window or bounces off a screen and flies away. However, sometimes they hit too hard and knock themselves unconscious for a bit. When they awaken they have to get their bearings on the back lanai or front porch before flying off. Tragically, there have been two occasions when birds broke their necks and died.

This day, I heard a splat on the kitchen window followed by a thump on the front porch. I knew a bird had hit hard and I was going to be surprised if it was alive. I went out to look and there he was: a thin yellow finch with touches of green. He was lying there and I could have sworn he had traded in his wings and chirp for angel wings and a harp. He was positioned on his back with one wing extended to his side and a leg jutting straight out on that same side. The other leg was crumpled up into itself. He had a little twitch to him, which I thought was his nervous system outliving the rest of his body.

I started talking to him, just saying, "You okay? Are you alive?" I gently petted him with my finger a couple of times to see if he would react. He didn't, but he was still twitching.

I weighed my options for what to do with his carcass. I settled on dropping it in the forest, but his neck kept twitching slightly. Then he moved his beak a little bit and I was like, 'Okay, the bird's definitely alive. I can't quit on him.'

I decided to jumpstart what was now my patient with a little meditation juice by sitting cross-legged next to the injured fella and letting the Will of Silence do whatever it needed to do. I didn't hold out too much hope but the thought crossed my mind that maybe it could bring him back from near death. Who knew what the limitations of this energy were? Or what the limitations of it acting through the limited vessel that is me were?

Not I. So I sat there and shut up. The Will of Silence maneuvered my hands around the bird without touching him. The hands did a bunch of quick gestures in the air. Nothing happened.

I sat there, worried that this wasn't going to work, the bird was too far gone. His back had to be broken along with one of those legs. I was mentally preparing myself to mercy kill him when an inspirational speech soared through my mind about how I can't kill him, that would be horrifying. This is a bird sanctuary. I'm resuscitating this bird!

The force within carried on with hand gestures and pantomime that ended in a loud clap. The finch responded by flipping over. Now he was sitting there with one tiny leg dangling between the wood planks of the porch. At least now he was upright.

Obviously, his back wasn't broken. I had assumed his leg was broken, but now I couldn't be sure. After flipping over he still wasn't moving, not even looking around, but the Will of Silence never stopped moving and gesturing in the space around him.

The finch grew more alert. He eventually did look around and gained his bearings. The whole time this was happening I heard his bird friends chattering amongst themselves in the trees, possibly trying to encourage him. I wondered if I weren't here would they be hopping around their friend trying to protect him or urging him to fly away with them?

Did they see the Will of Silence puppeteering me where I sat, and did they think, 'I dunno what all that's about, but this giant hasn't eaten our pal. We must take his message of friendship to our people!'

Upon hearing of us, did the bird people get that Carol and I were friendly and this was a sanctuary for them?

I didn't wonder those last two things in the moment. Back then, it would have been too self-involved. I save that for books.

The thin yellow finch was now on his belly and kind of half standing. His tail was a soft V-shape, reminiscent of a heart, but not quite. More like a kite. Probably some kites were patterned after this tail. His wings had a touch of orange to them, which I'd never seen before on these birds. He was darting his powdery green head this way and that, surveying his environment and looking at me, then looking around the porch. All the while I was thinking he must be a Volcano bird doing Air B&B here because his friends in the trees—the ones chattering away—had voices peculiar to that area.

Even though he was clearing his head it was obvious that my finch patient wasn't planning on abandoning the porch hospital. I was anxiously poring over what to do next since he clearly needed rehab. What sort of cage did we have to house him in while we nursed him back to health?

We had cat carriers that we'd used for injured ducks before, but I didn't think that would work for a finch. Would any wild bird respond well to a cat cage?

Carol said no. Mercifully, the Will of Silence sprang into action and so we never had to find out. It made my hand hover behind the finch in some sort of pose and then clapped twice. The bird responded by flying away, and that was it. Finchy Fincherton lived on. Our field hospital went back to being a normal front porch. Carol and I truly had created a bird sanctuary.

Well... with a caveat. See, being a sanctuary isn't all love and light like my extravagant story here makes it seem. There is an unspoken fact regarding our need for healing power in lieu of a vet: while we intend for our home to be a bird sanctuary, the windows are ours. That is to say, we didn't build this house but we live in it. And as with most houses, our house was erected to keep Nature out. To keep all "others" out, not just people.

We close the windows because we don't want mosquitos and birds flying through here. That poor finch wouldn't have smacked glass if we weren't here because no window would exist to fly into. There would be open skies like they expect. This speaks to the larger dilemma common to all in our society: we create the problems we solve and our solutions tend to create further problems, which we also then try to solve.

Please understand that birds would need neither a sanctuary nor a miracle healer if not for the inventions of humans. Also understand that when Carol and I say we're fostering a bird sanctuary we are focusing on the good we're doing. However, there is an unspoken shadow side to us acting on our best intentions, which is that we may always change our minds. Or we may move and the next tenants could destroy what we've built. The birds would suffer and we'd be fine. In creating this safe space for birds we cannot ignore who they need sanctuary from: us. All of us.

Reviving this tiny, precious finch energetically is a miracle. But, when you think about it, it's also a miracle that birds are still with us at all. Razing forests, killing off their homes, poisoning the air and the water and the plants and the insects—none of that is spiritual. Patting ourselves on the back for helping them survive us reinforces our specialness, our narcissism, and our phony role as stewards of Earth.

We have to remember that in the end, even with all of our do-gooding, we are harm. In maintaining our dysfunctional sense of self and society, we are harm. As long as we continue to normalize our completely bonkers separation from all that is, we are harm. In our attempting to create a sterile, pure, objective lens through which we view and judge life, we are harm.

That isn't to say it's bad to nurture and heal others harmed by us. It's good. It's better than consciously causing or ignoring suffering. It's good, but it's not great. It's not enough and never will be. It isn't human nature to be this harmful, although it is what we currently are. We're rowing on a turbulent sea that we set a massive wind turbine upon long ago and then forgot we did that. In our current state we are as natural as that.

Selling you on the healing properties of the Will of Silence would be harm atop harm. Don't buy it.

***

Days prior to the finch rescue I was out on the gazebo unleashing the meditation energy, which I hadn't done in a good long while. The weather forecast was predicting rain. I'd put off meditating for too long and didn't want to prance around out there when it was wet, because gross.

Lately, I had been obsessing over the question of what happens after physical death. While I was out there, I asked myself why I was unshakably focused on death. I was, after all, one who had the experience of being Ultimate Consciousness exploding the universe into existence from Nothing. I am someone who knows firsthand that there is more—far, far more—to us than meets the eye and materiality can produce.

Fear of death? Me? Why?

Is it because I am living as the self-awareness of timelessness decaying in time, fading out of being and into memory? Is that it? Sounds hoity-toity, yet that I can understand. With that, I further understand that understanding it doesn't stop it.

And so, as I was standing on the gazebo, eyes closed, Will of Silence dancing the body and placing it into magical postures, mind wondering what this fear of death was about, the bottom half of my vision turned from the normal eyelid blackness letting in sunlight's muddy redness to this beautiful white with a violet hue. The gazebo floor and ceiling were painted white, with neutrally stained wood posts holding the structure together. The roof and cupola were covered in green Ondura roofing, but that wasn't visible from inside. Since I was seeing white with violet notes in the bottom of my vision, I allowed that my eyes could be slightly open even though they felt tightly shut. Was I just seeing a mirage of white and violet caused by the floor in bright sunlight?

I'd never seen such before, but I couldn't rule it out. Seemed improbable mainly because even when I turned my head or my body to face where there was just the black lava rock outside the gazebo, the white and violet continued to be passively imagined with eyes closed.

I also very quickly realized that even though my arms were waving around and my hands were doing these poses in the air before me, I wasn't seeing any of it with eyes closed. So, I resolved, my eyes were not open even a peek. There indeed was this simple color scheme unlike any I'd seen in my mind's eye, and it had this peaceful vibe to it, a feeling that it had something to do with death.

Was this what near-death experiencers saw, the ones who talked about going to the light?

Nah. Probably not. That'd be too convenient.

The light show passed, and after more gestures and prancing about, the Will of Silence sat me on the gazebo stairs. I was just feeling my feelings, I guess you could say, and the feelings that came to mind were about our tabby cat, Oscar, dying. Specifically, the guilt I carried about how we had to put him to sleep. Isn't that supposed to be the guilt-free way of saying we had to kill him?

I had to keep reminding myself that the reason we had to put him to sleep was because he was doing so poorly. He wasn't eating. He was constantly throwing up. He was growing nonresponsive. Our once-vivacious cat who free-roamed the house had devolved into one who hid under a desk day and night, dying in slow motion and in a lot of pain.

We loved Oscar. We had to kill him.

As we drove him to the vet to pay her to murder him for us, he was extremely lucid, chipper, and curious the whole way. This was not like him at all. Oscar was deathly afraid of car rides, afraid of everything really, and this trip to the vet took about an hour.

No fear today. Of course not today, of all days. Best day of his life. Today, his final day, he was more alive than he had been since his body began rapidly failing him.

It was a warm and humid evening by the time the vet was done healing other people's sick animals and ready to kill our old boy. This was during the brief period when a majority of the country was taking the COVID-19 pandemic seriously. What that meant for us was that we could not be in the same room with the vet and vet tech, and therefore Oscar, when he died. We stood outdoors and stared through a large window as our guileless tabby lay on a table flanked by two strange humans pricking him with a needle that would bring him to his end.

As he died he looked sad and confused. Like he was aware enough to know what was happening to him. Like his confusion didn't stem from not knowing, because he could feel liquid death rushing through his veins. Like he didn't know how we could do this to him.

At least that's how I felt. I felt as though we had betrayed Oscar when really his sudden and, I am sure, temporary chipper lucidity had robbed us all of the sense that this was the only right decision.

After replaying that gut-wrenching day on the gazebo stairs, me-as-guilt switched focus to the one time Carol and I caught a rat in a glue trap in our garage. This was quickly becoming a greatest hits medley in my mind's eye of the death I hath wrought. This rat's death stood out because the glue trap didn't kill him the way you'd think it should, or else why buy one? As its name implies, the glue trap trapped him. In glue. Being stuck there afforded him all the time in the world to reflect on his mistakes in life and how he was going to rip me apart if I got too close.

Some people have no problem killing rats. I did. I liked rats. Just not in the garage because when last we had rats living there they burrowed into both of our cars and chewed through the wiring, including the drivetrain of the Honda. Their vehicular sabotage could have killed us. Fair is fair.

Or maybe it was mice. But still—fair is fair. Bird sanctuary. Not Ratsville.

This rat was only half caught in the glue trap. The bottom half, which meant that he was snapping and growling at me like a dog who wanted to tear my head off. I never knew rats growled. It was absurd and terrifying at the same time. I guess when you're trapped and you know you're going to die this is what you become. At least when you're a rat. And probably a human, too.

I got to work filling a bucket with hot water. My plan was to grab the rat with long tree branch clippers and dunk him like a witch until he drowned. I thought if the water was scalding hot it would be quick. I don't know why I thought that—maybe because he would want to scream instead of holding his breath thereby sucking in water faster.

When I came at the rat with the clippers he stopped snapping. He stopped growling. He started whimpering. And I, in my infinite wisdom, dexterity, and aim, missed him entirely and got the clippers stuck in glue. Reflexively, I dunked the clippers, rat, trap, and all, into in the bucket of water. I held it there until his last bubbles of breath surfaced indicating he died. Then held it there a few minutes longer in case he was faking it.

I have felt terrible about murdering the rat ever since. This wasn't some grungy, disgusting Manhattan sewer rat. This was a fluffy, sheen country rat. He was white like a lab rat. Maybe he descended from some escaped lab rats somewhere on the island, who knows?

What I learned about rats that day was that they are every bit as sentient as we are. Every bit as alive. Every bit as in love with life as we should be and as protective of themselves as I imagine any of us would be. I know reality is different than what I imagine, so that's the operative word: *imagine*.

Actually, the operative word is *I*, but why quibble?

Who was I to murder this pink-eyed four-legged white person for committing the cardinal sin of entering our garage in the middle of the sanctuary? If you can choose who you give sanctuary to, is it really a sanctuary?

As I slumped there on the stairs of the gazebo I started crying, thinking about our cat and thinking about this rat with his drastic change from snapping at me in the corner to pleading for his life. The outward, "I'm gonna get you! I'm gonna kill you! I'm gonna escape!" machismo reaction caved to his real feelings of terror and wanting to exist. Reliving it as I was, I bawled my eyes out there in the shadow of the gazebo's roof.

I didn't tell anyone, not even Carol, about the lights behind my lids or my breakdown while pondering animal murders because there are certain experiences that get cheapened by talking about them. It's like they're alive with personal meaning in the moment, and then when you retell them, they're degraded. Dead as a drowned rat. All of my experiences with the Intelligence of Silence feel this way.

Over time, of course, all experiences anyone has degrade to memory. The moment you're not in the moment but are in time trying to sling the past into the future to create a moment, your life is as cheapened as this sentence structure. And so now, since we're both here living on the cheap in time, I can fan my rarefied experiences before you like the Buddhist tchotchke display at an East Village flea market without feeling guilty.

Flea market spirituality, folks. I'm coining it.

***

Perhaps resuscitating the finch was selfish. Great for the bird, yes, but also good for me. Maybe after the lives I took I needed to have a win. Needed to rescue an animal, not just murder them. I think these issues of death and guilt were coming up for me in visceral ways because I needed to find that lightning strike of clarity through them that kills me once more. I became who I was by stripping away my personal psychological baggage until I realized that I never owned any. None of us do because all of us do. My baggage isn't mine, it's yours, too. And vice versa. We are in this sorrow together, all of us through all time and all cultures. When you come to that fact not intellectually and not because you remember Buddha talked about sorrow, but actually come to it? You are recontextualized out of solitary confinement as an alleged individual and into the collective where you belong.

Been there. Done that. Can't do it again, not in the same way. The same way is a memory. Trying to jumpstart a memory will only leave me in memory.

As I say all of this for the umpteenth time, I realize that it's not as though I don't have human feelings anymore. I feel, it's just that I have way more self-awareness about my feelings as illusions now. Whenever I feel down in the dumps I immediately surface in the lifejacket of realization that this isn't real. Not in the depressed, "None of this is real, maaaaan!" way of conspiracy mind or emo songs, but in the way that only firsthand experience of the real impresses upon you.

How does *that* guy wake up out of the remnants of his self yet again?

I suspect I can't know until it—whatever it is—clicks and I am properly contextualized again. After the fact, when Jer 2.0 is behind me, I will know what happened. Not glued to a trap of thoughts on the gazebo, gazing across the lava field in confusion about death and life, but when I look for and expect nothing.

Perhaps spontaneously while feeding ducks?

Not now that I've said it. Now it would be a projection —the angel out in front of me trailing desire.

I need to feed the ducks either way. They have no illusions about living in illusion, and they always know when it's dinnertime. Another miracle?

Timelessness is not for the birds.

Chapter 16
The Gazebo

Carol and I were not super wealthy when we moved here. I had zero money and she had some money with zeroes in it. When she sold her Brooklyn apartment she had just enough to make this work for us. I still had zero. We searched high and low, quite literally, up and down three volcanos on Hawaii Island for the perfect place, the place that spoke to us, inviting us in. I mean that quite literally, too.

We looked at numerous houses located in different states of human population ranging from quaint town to golfing community to near-complete isolation. Of all the places we looked only two spoke to us. Well... not including the golfing community—although it wasn't the land that spoke to us there. It was the old White people wearing plastic smiles and waving at us as we tore through at a mean 15 miles per hour. They gave that creepy, robotic vibe only advantaged Whites emit. It's the one that says, "Welcome!" And beneath that pleasantry, "I'm seething with misplaced rage! Be White, too! Property values! Aloha!"

There was a beautiful place we checked out in Captain Cook, an isolated off-grid house in the middle of an old growth forest up mauka—up the mountain. Funny enough, the ancient Ōhi'a trees there told us to get out, too, just like the elderly golf course Whites, minus the fake smiles. Maybe the trees didn't like that I was the privileged White invader in this instance. Carol is Chinese-American. She's less of an invader but invasive nonetheless. I can't take all the blame.

Whatever the reason, we both felt the vibe. It was direct. The location was idyllic, but, man, those Ōhi'a trees simply did not want humans living there. I couldn't blame them, though. We heard chainsawing not far from us.

The other place where the land spoke our names was here, where we live now. This place greeted us with a childlike vibe. Here was happy to see us. Here wanted us to feel with it its own specialness. 17 1/2 acres of diverse life: sky-scraping windbreaker trees, all manner of citrus, avocado, mango, a plot of rainbow eucalyptus—and that's just the trees. The place felt enchanting and imaginative. I don't know how to say it in a way that translates. All I can tell you is we both felt it. This place called out to us when we left.

How does one afford 17 1/2 acres and a nice house in Hawaii without owning Facebook, you ask? Well, I don't know that they do anymore. Far too many people ran from the COVID pandemic to the islands, which jacked up the prices. But back in 2016, when we moved in, our place was relatively inexpensive. Seven acres of flattened lava field played into that. To us, barren lava is visually striking and deeply magical, but to many it's considered "useless" land. Can't farm it. Can't build another house on it because of zoning restrictions. What can you do with it?

Hey, how about appreciate it for the raw Nature that it is? For the feeling you get walking out to this quiet, windy, magical expanse of fire frozen in time?

To me the lack of interest and lack of astonishment at the drastic, instant change in terrain is like walking on the back of a dragon and shrugging it off as, "Meh. Dragons." The black lava field bordering lush greenery is death bordering life, except this death also shows signs of life. Not ghosts in this case but ferns and trees struggling to claim it for themselves.

At first we didn't want to build anything on the lava field. We loved its pristine nature, the naked power of its visual statement. But I followed the advice of my friend, Tiokasin Ghosthorse, and asked the land if it would be okay to build an unobtrusive gazebo on it. The land said, "Sure, Jer. Whatever you want." And I was like, "Oh, you sound just like me! How convenient!" The land said, "Right?" We shared a laugh and then Carol and I had a gazebo built there.

The gazebo was held together with strong ʻōhiʻa posts. Probably from the bastard forest that rejected us. I made a snaking river of a path to it out of wood chips with a blue rock border. All told, it looked like something Hobbits might live in.

About a year after it was finished Carol and I got married on it. About a year after that I began collaborating out there with the Intelligence of Silence.

Many are the mornings that I walk out to the gazebo in my fancy flip flops, called *slippahs* in Hawaii, to meditate. Not every morning, not religiously, but often. And at first it was just that, just meditation, which for me means allowing the Will of Silence to freely do what it must through this here body.

The open lava field is super windy, and we don't have screens or windows on the gazebo, so it's all open air. There are, however, benches along the periphery. When it wasn't dancing the body around and posing, the Will of Silence would do basic stretches and exercises utilizing the benches in ways that I would never have imagined. If I were twisting my spine around a bench consciously, unconsciously, or delusionally, I would have broken myself by now. But not the Will of Silence. It knew just what to do and when. Always knew how best to work for the greater good of all, including me. It stretched me out, cracked my back, and cracked my neck, making me healthier and more pliable. It undid the damage I had caused during the day and in the night from sleeping on my sides too much.

There are healthy ways to sleep, healthy ways to lie down, to sit up, to stand, to walk, and the Intelligence of Silence knows them all. I only know how to hurt myself like a baby in a man body. I suspect I am not alone in this. Those of us who can walk were taught how to remain upright so that our feet moved us from point A to point B without those goofy ape hands galloping us. We were not taught beyond that. Perhaps we couldn't be taught more without a voice that is us and not us instructing us further, or the Will of Silence leading by example. Without, in other words, the aid of an invisible intelligence who sees the impact of even our most basic visible movements on both the seen and unseen world around us, as well as the relationship those perspectives of the environment have on us. We live in relationship with the invisible whether we know it or not. I'm not talking about religion, I'm talking about walking down the street.

So that was what I initially started doing out there: feeling the environment and allowing the Intelligence of Silence to do as it willed. Gaining flexibility and balance. Learning to stand, walk, and dance with the wind.

Meanwhile, back in the house, I began asking the Intelligence of Silence if it could heal others. The Will of Silence would take over and do just that, working on whatever was ailing Carol or our kitties at the time. I knew from previous experience that this energy had some ability to heal, although I had no idea it could heal animals.

I have no want to be a healer. If I want anything it is for everybody to go through this transformation, too, and be the healing they seek. I don't want to spend my life as a crutch for people who refuse to walk and will just keep breaking themselves. I do enough of that on my own. That said, as miraculous as this healing capability seems, it is not, as far as I can tell, a cure-all, and it often takes a longer route to healing than how you may travel with a doctor or other medical professional.

For instance, if you have a specific pain in a specific location, you will naturally want that body part worked on. Well, this energy may agree with you or it may not. It will work on problems that you may not even know you have and will often prioritize them over what you want healed in the first place. The Will of Silence decides the order of importance for healing your ailments. You don't even need to tell me what's bothering you for it to work on you.

Also, when necessary, it will work on certain parts of the body that seem unrelated to the problem. Lo and behold, you will find that they are connected. Sometimes you receive instantaneous healing from this bodywork. Sometimes it takes a little bit of sleep afterwards. Maybe a lot of sleep. Maybe you'll wake up the next morning and be all better. But sometimes you won't be all better, you'll be a lot better, and it will take several sessions. It probably depends on the ailment and I don't know that it can heal everything.

The Intelligence knows how to work whatever the systems are that we already understand, whether it be reiki, acupressure, massaging the fascia, qigong, or any other modality you can name. I'm not a specialist in any of these things. I don't know much about them. I'm shocked I used the word *modality* just now. But the Will of Silence uses elements from all sorts of modalities to heal and is their master.

Back when I was first playing with this I wondered if it could heal long distance. Could I make the gazebo a healing center and then just ask to heal the cats, or Carol, or whomever, from out on the lava field? Is there such a thing as a place that holds and distributes directed healing energy? Or is such reserved for, like, nuclear reactors and power plants?

It's interesting: since I have access to these capabilities you'd think it would dawn on me to ask for more, to keep playing with it, to even follow through on what I had resolved to do, building a healing center in the gazebo. But my followthrough wasn't great. More times than not when I was out there I would forget to ask if it was possible. When I would ask it was more of an afterthought. It was like something in me said, "Eh. Forget about it. We've got bigger tofu fish to fry."

Those bigger tofu fish were usually Hawaii herself in terms of just asking, "How can I help Hawaii?" Or, "How can I help the land?" Because to step out onto that lava field and stand between the peak of Mauna Loa and the roaring Pacific Ocean, and feel the wind on your face, and on your entire body, really, with the drastic tropical sun, and with the lack of human voices and technological noise, with the birds chirping and filling that quiet, with distant cows mooing and filling that quiet—feeling the quiet and feeling the natural sounds filling the quiet at the same time—the full sensory snapshot brings you invariably to a state of thankfulness wherein you wish to be of service. Service to the land and the air and the sea and to the spirit of here. That's a lot of what I ended up doing.

Whether or not the gazebo can be a healing center in the way I had thought to ask is still up in the air. Perhaps literally. And again, that's all I am doing is asking. Usually, I'm asking what this energy can do to help and then the energy will dance me accordingly. Often, within those moments, it will work on my physical and psychic ailments as well. Whatever is broken in me is integrated within the healing dance for the environment at large, for I am an element of the environment, too.

I'm not just Jeremy out on a gazebo doing a wonky little two-step in humble thankfulness. I am that humble thankfulness. I am that snapshot, which is promoting the feeling and is that feeling. The feeling is not merely translated through me. It is there. It is palpable. It is in the air and it is the air, and I am also that.

And so I wonder, now, if I gave up on the project of turning the gazebo into a healing center on my own, or if the question shrivels and dies every time I enter the state of thankfulness because it's deceivingly small? A small thought that believes it's bigger than it is. A thought not coming from that transcendent place. The place that sees you totally. The place that is you. The place out of reach and out of sight of those who can only theorize and babble about it.

Maybe.

Or maybe I should revisit the idea next time I'm out there. But it just feels fanciful. It feels like there are limits and that's the limit.

Or maybe I'm putting the limit on it. Maybe it isn't a real limit. Maybe it only feels like wish fulfillment. Writing this is silly enough. Unless I'm wrong and it works.

Eh, maybe I'll try after I finish this book and if I mysteriously forget to try again, or lose interest for no apparent reason while I'm out there, I'll know the question is a noise that burns away the closer it gets to the energy of Silence.

Okay, fine. It's settled. I should experiment with it more, and I will. If anything noteworthy comes of it I'll share. But I didn't do much with it then. Then, I turned to something even more preposterous.

***

We live in a wildfire hazard zone. Our home is not hooked up to municipal water; we collect rain in a catchment tank. This is probably one of the other reasons the land didn't sell for years until we bought it. We've got to catch rain from the roof and store it in a 19,000 gallon tank, then pump it through a proper filtration system so we don't die drinking it. For all of that to work we need a good many downpours or else we'll be paying to have water trucked in before the tank runs dry. Carol and I needed to know if the Will of Silence could make rain.

It's not as eye-roll-worthy a request as it sounds. How many First Nations peoples make rain, including Kānaka Maoli on this very island? Surely, such dances are also tools for the Will of Silence. And so I asked if it's possible to make rain.

Short answer: Yes.

Long answer: How would you like that served?

Turns out there are a slew of ways to make rain, although I doubt any of what the Intelligence of Silence was willing this body to pantomime looked like rain dances. Sometimes there were dance-like movements involved, but they were elements of a larger performance, not the full show.

The body was used in different ways to make different types of rain. One type, which took the longest and produced the least, was forming puffy, rounded clouds out of thin air and making a choo-choo train of them, one puff after another after another. They manifested from a single point in the sky, arced around our house, and then melded together. That newly-formed cloud mass produced rain. This was the most dramatic and most strenuous means of calling in the sky tears.

A second way was to take cloud cover moving in off the mountain, and also off the ocean, and merge them over the house. This produced more rain than the cloud train puffing along, but it didn't usually last more than one night. It tended to produce rain later that evening and no longer. Sometimes just a spitting of it. Not so useful.

At some point in my experimenting I had the bright idea to do the thing I should have been doing all along: observe what these movements were saying. Some of them have a story to tell. Though I cannot translate them in whole, parts of them are obvious. Like, for instance, having my fingers pantomime rain tinkling down to the ground or motioning up to the sky. When I saw the up to the sky routine, I thought, 'Oh, what if I should ask the land and the trees for help?'

So I did. And I do. But not in the selfish, "Will you help me?" way. It's more like, "Do you want to be a part of this? Can we do this together?

"I'm here for you. I'm trying to make rain for you. For the catchment tank, yes, and also for the ducks. For the plants and the trees and the pigs. For the land. We're all in this together. Can we do this?"

Later I learned of the Hawaiian proverb, "Hahai no ka ua i ka ululā'au," which translates to, "The rain follows the forest." When it comes to working with Nature I strongly suspect that all of what I think are my personal bright ideas are just me catching on to what Hawaiians already know.

My next bright idea was to ask the wind for help. Specifically, I wanted to know if we could (or should) change the direction of the wind to blow hard from the ocean side, because it seemed to me that the best way to make long-lasting rain would be to call in clouds from the ocean. Not just the band of clouds that I see going around the island, because that very well may be volcanic fog, or *vog*, from Kilauea, which is in a frequent state of eruption. I assumed there had to be storms, clouds, or the potential for such further out over the sea that we could call in for the trees to draw down. With all of my allies ready to go I yielded the body to the Will of Silence and we began the process of blowing clouds inland to capture the rain.

It worked. As childish a lie as this may sound to many a reader, doing this produced days of rain, fending off tinderbox drought. Ten days of sunshine predicted by my phone's weather app and the friendly weatherperson on KHON2 News went down the tubes with a little ask, a little dance, and a lot of mahalos. I'd meditate in the morning and by early to mid evening we'd have rain for days.

If I had to guess at a success rate, I'd put it at 98% and arguably 100%. It's arguable because I believe that 2% of the time the Will of Silence knew not to bother with my request, for rain was coming on its own within a week. That, or it was calling in rains from way out in the ocean that would take a few days to arrive. I suspect the former because that's in line with how it treats healing: the Intelligence knows whether or not we actually need what we're asking. With rain, 2% of the time it's telling me, *Just wait*.

If ever I had a doubt that this energy moving the body was producing effects in the environment, which I did—I did believe in coincidences, after all—the Intelligence gave a demonstration that challenged the odds of coincidence. Carol and I had a friend who was walking on a beach down the road. I had just gotten done meditating out on the gazebo where the Will of Silence performed in a way characteristic of when I lived in New York. It spun the body really fast in a circle, like doing a Whirling Dervish twirl. However, the accompanying arm and hand gestures were different than the Dervish twirls. I had a feeling that these twirls were connected with the weather because they occurred in the middle of the Will of Silence telling the story of making it rain, if you want to call it that. (Again, it's not exactly dancing but it is exactly telling the story of an ask and preparing the environment for rain.) In the middle of this the Will of Silence spun me around dizzyingly fast while making mudras with the hands, and I jokingly thought, 'I hope I'm not making a tornado.'

Later that day, at 4:50 p.m. to be exact, our friend on the beach texted me that a funnel cloud was churning down South Point. He sent an accompanying picture of a long waterspout winding up the beach. Waterspouts are rare in Hawaii and he, a lifelong beach dweller, had never seen one on land.

Did the Will of Silence create this semi-long distance show for our friend to report to us? Or did it dance the dance of a waterspout that it knew was destined to form where it did so that when our friend saw it and inevitably texted us we would make the association? I have no conclusion there, but the end result would have been the same.

***

So that's the story of the gazebo. It is a place of union. A place of healing. It is a place of creating moisture in a dry, fire-prone land.

Our newest neighbors who know nothing about my sweet, natural, communion moves commented on how weird it is that we get more rain than they do even though they reside higher up in elevation than we. I didn't know this until they said it. Technically, they should be getting slightly more rain than we do, or at least the same amount. And I assumed my little rain asks brought everyone in the area magic waters. Nope. So maybe I need to expand the ask and help them out, too.

Then again, they're on municipal water, so screw them. Let them have their own selfless death and come back to selfishly make rain.

Ah, transcendence. Ain't it spiritual?

Chapter 17
In The Yard

Growing up a city boy, my idea of home was a rented apartment that may or may not have included a small, easily distinguished, fenced-in yard. Can a sprawling 17 1/2 acre expanse really be considered a yard? Given that our house isn't plopped down in the center, does it even have a front and a back?

It's hard to think of this place as ours, but the self-centered English language I speak, the concept of our home being the center of our property, and our mortgage bills, certainly help. When I think of our backyard I think of everything behind the house, which is simple enough because it's mostly an open field with a side cluster of trees—mango, neem, avocado, and monkey pod. When I think of our front yard I think of the small area immediately out our front door, which is delineated by a raised rock garden. The land beyond the garden consists of fields, orchards, a workshop, and the lava field, all of which are sectioned off by windbreaker trees and the lava rock berm. When I talk about mowing it I'll knowingly and ironically say, "I'm going to mow the lawn." Really, it's the daunting task of keeping razor grass that grows taller than me low enough to drive over without accidentally mowing small boulders the island keeps spitting up to test my focus like Donkey Kong.

These are my boundaries. This is my language and my way of conventionalizing the land in terms of property.

Not necessarily Carol's and certainly not the ducks'. Definitely not the feral pigs'. In fact the pigs think it's their lawn and we're squatting in their house.

The truth is, everywhere is for everyone. To create an interior space for ourselves is to defend a spot against everyone else with sealant, traps, and repellents. The very structure itself with walls, a floor, and a roof, is a defense mechanism. I'm not saying houses are bad or by any means advocating against them. I'm pointing out that even healthy boundaries are definitionally defense mechanisms, and as far as Nature at large is concerned, everywhere is for everyone.

Including invisible everyones.

Before we go there let's start at a place most of us are more comfortable with when considering the great outdoors: Nature documentaries. Some of us don't enjoy stepping outside of our homes, preferring to stare at Nature in all her glory from the glory of the couch. Sure, when we watch documentaries we're only engaging two of our senses: sight and sound. And, yes, we're listening to a narrator interpret what we're seeing and hearing. But that sure beats mosquitos and sneezing.

Two problems arise with Nature doc narration scripts. They're the same problems shared with all the science being done on, to, and with, Nature by everyone in zoology, earth sciences, and even by naturalists: although the filmmakers are documenting natural relationships, they don't consider relationship to be an intrinsic and hugely important factor in the act of observing the living. And they don't consider the dead.

The average Nature doc narrator speaks in cold, impersonal tones to describe, and therefore interpret, what we're seeing. Now, I ask you, does "cold and impersonal" reflect the actual world you live in or the animal that you are? It cannot because of this little thing called *relationship*.

Relationship happens spontaneously and immediately when you enter a new environment or come upon new beings. Every living being that comprises the environment is responding to your presence, just as you are doing. Truth be told, there is no new environment that you're stepping into. The moment you're there you are also a being in and of the environment. The idea that you are somehow different than wherever you are located because you've never been there before may afford you either a feeling of security as an explorer or, conversely, a feeling of insecurity as one who is afraid of the unknown. But make no mistake: everywhere you touch, Earth is comprised of living beings making conscious and unconscious decisions about you and you about them. You're not alone in gawking and watching your step. Presence is relationship.

In actual living Nature, personal views play the biggest role in the environment because relationship is how the environment functions. One could say that the Will of Nature is enacted through innumerable relationships. Impersonally, we know this as the web of life. Impersonally, we talk about a food chain as the hierarchy of animal dominance. Impersonally, we talk about instinct and primal drives. Talking about Earth and all her inhabitants impersonally is like concentrating on the organs, processes, and systems within your body while ignoring the reason for all of those "mechanical" relationships in the first place: you and the life you live.

Can we talk about how we really are with each other? How we truly are day to day in our thinking about and walking with Nature?

Why do we make those documentaries at all given that they are documenting a lie? The lie of the cold, impersonal observer taking in a scene objectively. That's not who animals are. Plants are. That's not who we are and we are Nature, too.

We fantasize our divorce because the Bible assures us that God created us in his image and all this other life is just some crap for us to do with as we please. Yeah, sure, it would be nice if we were stewards of the rock we live on, but turning a profit is nice, too. Dominating others feels good, too. Sterile information delivery feels civilized and above Nature's consciousness.

When you're crazy.

Wherever you live, consider your environment right now. Is there a tree you rescued from a strangling vine? What do you feel from the tree when next you meet?

From a stray cat you fed that one time and he keeps coming back?

An owl you nursed to health and now more owls come around?

A stray dog you tried to approach in your own way, without listening to what her needs were, and she bit you?

Those red ants that climbed up your shoe, rode you home, and scouted your pantry for their next meal?

From deer in the yard inching closer for longer the more you don't react to their presence?

A mouse trying to set up a condominium for family in your walls? Does she tread lightly or boldly dart into the living room while you're watching?

What do you feel from a sad houseplant you water to death as it creeps toward the window that gets all the sun?

The manic hamster you feed poorly and keep locked in a cage you barely clean because when you used to try to pick him up and nuzzle him he bit you?

From the puppy you let your child innocently torture with a strangling hug because you think it's cute?

The pets you purposely torture because you lack empathy and they're just animals?

The dog you never let inside because he's an outdoor dog?

The tropical fish you keep confined to a tank so you can feel meditative staring at them when you get home from work and need to relax?

From the bumblebees you would welcome if you didn't have a deadly allergy to their sting?

The rattlesnake sunbathing in your driveway?

The massive cockroach clicking out an alert by the sugar in the kitchen cabinet?

The earthworm you rescued from a dirty puddle on your concrete walkway after that massive thunderstorm?

Wherever you live and whoever you are there is an ecosystem several layers deep in which you are embedded. What do you feel from your extended family of water, earth, and sky neighbors—including the encroaching creepy uncles with more legs and eyes than any living being should have? Not feel *for* them, but *from* them? Have you ever listened to them that way?

And there's more.

When we're talking about the yard we're talking about personal space—yours and every organism's overlapping. So it matters who the person is creating personal space, no? If ducks and pigs and silverfish are already who they need to be—if they fully express the consciousness of their species—well, what about you? What do you express?

Self interest? Relational interest? A combination? What about the Will of Silence? Ya got that going or what?

Who you are not only helps determine the type of relationship you're going to have with other organisms, but also with beings comprising the invisible landscape. There is more to the yard than just its quantifiable contents. There is Mystery. And Mystery includes the dead.

The dead as still-functioning entities are a part of capital "M" Mystery. You can be selfish as hell and still encounter them. How you encounter them, as well as whether or not you unravel them from capital "M" Mystery as standalone phenomena, depends on the flavor of mind you are expressing. No doubt from my wordplay, encounters with spectres take place along a spectrum. The feelings we have about the dead in our vicinity and our encounters with them affect the yard.

For example, if you've ever buried a beloved pet in the yard, think about how that altered the space. It became a hallowed ground for you, didn't it?

When you visit the graves of the deceased who mean something to you, there comes an air of the sacred. A certain quietude takes you over and takes over that area of the yard as personal meaning seeps into the "impersonal" environment. You contribute a palpable feeling to that spot. Others may feel the special vibe without you telling them anyone is buried there.

If you live in an apartment, or otherwise do not have a yard, you're not immune to the dead. Perhaps grandma passes away and comes to you in a dream. If that type of experience happening to you wasn't on your radar, guess who just fried your radar?

And now you'll treat nighttime differently. The dark differently. Your bedroom differently. Oh, you'll be obsessing over grandma and whether that really happened or if it was just a dream for years to come. It won't help matters if you see fleeting glimpses of what looks like her robe flitting by in whichever room was her favorite.

Speaking of, was that Cuddle Kitty who just ran past you in the hallway? That beautiful orange furball died one year ago today. How she loved bounding down the hall. I wonder if the other cats saw her, too. They seem to be acting stranger than normal.

Death works on you and you, in turn, work on the environment, if only just a little bit. If only to create a sacred spot outdoors or paranormal activity indoors. See how it doesn't matter if the origins are a dream in your head where the dead reach out to you or if you create an atmosphere in a specific location where you feel them? When your feelings change, the room changes. The yard changes. And when others comment on the feeling of the place in question, that's humbling validation.

Those are examples of how we as Westerners, raised to be self-centered and unconscious of the dead all around us, except as a topic for debate, a taboo to whisper, a dark force to fend off with light, a stupid thing ignorant people believe in, or a personal experience to only share with people whom we trust will not mock us, view the most palatable, i.e., socially acceptable, beings of the invisible ecology around us. But what about natural cultures not reprogrammed by old religious books men wrote to control the populations of their day? How might their understanding of death affect the places they live? How might they live alongside beings and formless awarenesses who dip in and out of their perception?

III

SPREAD YOUR WINGS AND FLAP

"Thesis is followed by antithesis, and between the two is generated a third factor, a lysis which was not perceptible before. In this the psyche once again merely demonstrates its antithetical nature and at no point has really got outside itself.

"In my effort to depict the limitations of the psyche I do not mean to imply that only the psyche exists. It is merely that, so far as perception and cognition are concerned, we cannot see beyond the psyche."

- Dreams, Memories, Reflections, Carl Jung

Chapter 18
Leapin' Lizards

Geckos. I love our little lizard pals. Every evening three to five brown geckos crawl around the outside of our kitchen window eating anything with wings. It's like having a gecko aquarium for free.

In the day, bigger green geckos come out to play... with our cats. There are two that hang out on the lanai just outside the sliding glass doors. There, they taunt Alfie and especially Sir Palm Trees. Many are the afternoons when you will catch Sir Palm Trees trying to pry the door open to get at the lizards darting in and out of wood slats. I mean, they are right there! So close and yet so far.

When I go to clean the duck run in the morning I am sometimes treated to a rare mourning gecko sighting on the roof of one of the doghouses. I was told by numerous locals that these are Hawaiian geckos and they're being driven to extinction by larger invasive green geckos who eat them. While it's true they are being threatened, I've seen a lot of pushback on their status as Hawaiian geckos because, technically, the mourning gecko was brought here 1,500 years ago by Polynesians. We are supposed to believe that they are just as unHawaiian as, say, the gold dust day gecko, which illegally smuggled here and spread across the islands in 1974.

Setting this standard for what it means to be Hawaiian is a White people thing. It's a product of the colonizer mindset. If geckos from 1500 years ago aren't Hawaiian then neither are the Polynesians who canoed here. Another way to say it is, White people of today are just as Hawaiian as Hawaiians because if you go back far enough you'll find that none of us are native to the islands. This is how Whites of the colonizer mindset who move here alleviate whatever guilt they feel in destroying the place by making it as polluted and depleted as they are. Making it feel how they feel inside. Making it feel like home.

The problem with their pretending that centuries upon centuries of living here is the same as a few decades to make the point that no one belongs anywhere, therefore I belong wherever I want to go, is that being Hawaiian isn't just about being the original people here or the Tahitians who immigrated next. It's about the fact that those peoples, once here, melded with the land and the sea and the sky. Their new culture, rooted in Earth, grew through them and birthed into the world what it means to be Hawaiian. It's not just about being first, it's about being family. It's about living in love with where you are so deeply that it is who you are. This doesn't mean there are no conflicts, no wars, even, between people. It means you're never at war with Earth. You take care of Earth as Earth takes care of you. It means becoming Hawaii.

And you know who knows that? Hawaiian mourning geckos. They have adapted since arriving on these shores some 1,500 years ago. They don't demand that Hawaii adapt to them. They're not white enough for that level of narcissism.

***

Shortly after moving here Carol and I had the great privilege of being introduced to Willie Iaukea. We became steadfast friends. He was my best man at our wedding out on the gazebo. I was his confidante and student of sorts. I have learned more about original Hawaiian life, culture, origin of folklore, and the peoples' origin story from Willie than any course the University of Hawaii could offer.

Willy is a kapuna, a Hawaiian elder and keeper of his family's lineage of knowing, which extends all the way back to the original inhabitants of the Island of Hawaii. Willie explains what makes sacred sites here feel sacred. Not why they are considered sacred, which may or may not be related, but why some of them feel alive with their own vibrant energy that people often interpret as haunted or alive with spirit. It is, to put it crudely, because in the original way of doing things someone volunteered to protect the location in death until such time as a family member released them from their kuleana—their responsibility. When Westerners came with their deadly diseases and even deadlier Christianization, outlawing Hawaiian dance, chants, language, their very being Hawaiian, the knowledge of such pacts was largely lost. As a result, few family members left knew to release these spirits.

That may sound like a sad allegory about colonization, but it is the actual. Hawaiians understand that family does not just extend all the way back in time; their ancestors are also right here, right now. And while their sense of time may seem curious to we linear people, it was, and as they regain their cultural identity, is, the way people inhabited the seen world and the invisible world around them. Just as our sense of time dictates our focus, informing how we look at the world, exist in the world, create in the world, experience limitations, and so forth, so, too, with nonlinear people. Think of how their inclusivity of the dead as family members living in another form right here, right now, doesn't just inform what we would call their religious rituals and beliefs, but informs all aspects of their actual experience. How they invent. How they dream. How they move with Earth. What duties they take up in the afterlife.

Westerners may accept or reject their culture's religious rituals and beliefs, which, again, are based on old accounts written and compiled by men. Religion and personal choice are the only reference points we have for understanding how natural cultures live spiritually. We call them *religious practitioners* and *cultural practitioners* because that's what we have in our society: people who choose to practice their religion. People who may choose to adopt different cultural beliefs. And now (or perhaps *for* now) we Americans won't be tortured and killed for speaking against the fiction language of our dominating pseudo culture.

Because we transpose our meanings onto everyone else, we never really hear Hawaiians or understand them. We never understand them as us. Where they are inclusive, we are exclusive. This affords us the cancerous privilege to, for instance, speak platitudes about respecting Hawaiian religious practitioners while deciding to plop another massive telescope atop their sacred volcano, Mauna Kea.

We think their culture is adorable. We clap at their performances. But when it comes to promoting a view of how the world works and what is important in life, that's when it's time for the Westernized adults in the room to assert their maturity and their dominance once again, because learning factoids about deep space is more important to our evolution than just... you know... believing something. Practicing something. Something dead to us. Something that was never alive in our pseudo culture to begin with.

We Westerners firmly believe in things, too, but we call them facts. The word gives us permission to ignore the actual fact that they are largely beliefs. We believe that information is evolution and since time is an arrow, evolution is what we must do. We must imitate physical evolution through psychological time. Those people playing ancestral dress-up are cute and all, but they're backwards. Only science is forward-thinking.

Again, Hawaiians, natural cultures at large, are not practicing religion. They are not practicing customs. This is not a dress rehearsal. We are condescending.

They are inhabiting the world they understand just as we are, only they don't suffer the same limitations we do because they don't edit the world around them the way we do. First, we had to edit the world to fit a religious mold or we could be killed. Now, we edit anything we deem to be religious out of the world because of that trauma. We are right to deprogram ourselves from religious repression and intolerance, but we're wrong to transfer that repression and intolerance onto other cultures who never were religious to begin with. Like our scientists, they were observant. And they behaved accordingly.

Westerners are geniuses in their single-minded focus, but it comes at a price: their soul. And with that, understanding the souls all around them. The souls moving through them. The landscape of souls.

State-sponsored Roman religion deemed it taboo to talk about souls around you as a way of destroying European natural cultures with Christianity. Ancestors remaining all around us as guides and guardians whom we become in death was replaced with our escaping to heaven or hell when we die—or to purgatory, until that became unfashionable. Any entity claiming to be an ancestor was deemed a trick of the devil.

Now, instead of reconsidering the worldviews of people repressed and displaced by religion, the scientific and materialist mind has largely decided that book religions rebranded the unreal, backwards, and illogical beliefs of natural cultures with their own version. Scientists don't generally view themselves as a repressive furtherance of the priestly class because in many respects the world authentically "works" the way scientific findings conclude. Inconveniently, however, part of the way reality appears to work so coherently is by glossing over the fact that through never-ending scientific discoveries, the rules of what works keep changing. They ignore this by accounting for it. By lauding it, actually, as "the beauty of science." As in, "The beauty of science is that it is open to new discoveries."

Except, apparently, the one that comes from a long look in the mirror.

When we collapse the ecology of formless awarenesses inhabiting the land and moving through us into belief, we not only condescend to the original peoples we were before we deluded ourselves with brainwashing books courtesy of the Roman Empire—not only condescend to the natural peoples who either never deluded themselves or are awakening from that delusion right now—we are, in our reinventing space/time, keeping ourselves from adulthood in that larger invisible ecology. And so, when we have encounters with invisible beings, we misunderstand them. We're told they aren't real, so we have to grasp at them from the periphery of our knowledge of religion, myth, archetypes, folklore, and so on. Or we perform the same pseudoscience over and over, such as recording EVPs so that we can boast about spirits yammering at us from the ether. This gives us a sense of repeatability, which we hope will translate to respectability amongst the high priests of science. But it never fosters respectability. It can't. It can only call attention to how wrong their view of space/time is, and that's a big no-no.

It's fine for scientists and academics to eternally make new discoveries and new hypotheses within their self-contoured reality bubble, but bursting their bubble ain't an option. Expanding their bubble is evolution. Popping it is death. Imagine dying and discovering the world of souls you've been hiding from. Eek.

The hitch is that we cannot repress forever. And now we have the technological means to invent grotesque computerized mutations of what we actually are—the actuality we've been repressing. Understanding what drives us to invent such things can wake us up if we choose to see them as us holding a mirror to ourselves. Or they can destroy us if, like Narcissus, we fall in love with what we see, which is what we're doing now.

If you are a tech bro prone to baulking at word arrangements like "ecology of souls," please tell us again about how the goal of your life's work is to upload humanity into computer cloud storage. This "new" thought you have been working on is an unhealthy repackaging of how things already are.

See what I mean?

And there's more.

Even when we do want to know the dead; even when we hunt them; even when they materialize before us with a prophesy or a farewell, we do not really understand what we're encountering because our modern culture never included them to be understood. It may be that some natural cultures don't understand the dead either, even if they have a unified cultural lens through which to process encounters. But from what I have seen, they have observed and interacted with spirits and the "spirit world" for so long, and so openly, that they know the difference between legitimate encounters and fantasy. Pre-Western Hawaiians, for example, didn't believe that every dream was a message and every nightmare an omen from beyond. They understood that dreams had multiple sources. Some were normal personal dreams, some normal nightmares. Some nightmares, they knew, were brought on by eating goatfish, which contain a hallucinogenic toxin in their heads—yes, that specific and "scientific." And some, they knew, some were messages from ancestors.

They also understood the differences in non-dream visions, non-dream encounters with ancestors, prophesies from ancestors, on and on. Pretty sophisticated classifications for a supposedly prelogical society.

Western mind believes it is logical when in actuality it is still transitioning from prelogical to logical. Translogical looks like prelogical until the logical mind creeps up on the facts and discovers otherwise for itself. We have yet to catch up with the various natural cultures who see us clearly because they've been where we are in a previous loop on the time spiral. They are who we will become like if we survive ourselves in this one. Unless or until we do resolve our having deviated from the natural we will continue to arrogantly deem natural cultures prelogical, which is a modern racist way of saying, *inferior*—a term the inclusive natural cultures would never use for anyone.

***

We will not come to understand the invisible ecology in which we are enmeshed on its terms with our braggadocios toddler mind. Therefore, we will never fully understand ourselves. I can think of no more dramatic an example of this than my brief time spent at a mass grave site located nowhere near our yard: my couple of weekends in Gettysburg, Pennsylvania back in 2010.

Gettysburg is a place famous for two things. First, the Battle of Gettysburg, which was the bloodiest battle in the Civil War. With over 51,000 deaths in three days, this battle is considered the turning point of the war. Oh, and second, for being one of the most haunted lands on Earth thanks to said battle.

To this day people travel to Gettysburg from all around the globe to participate in war reenactments by day and hunt ghosts of the actual actors by night. Much can be said about the role of liminality in paranormal activity on display here. Much can also be said about how obsessively fetishizing this battle through dressing up as soldiers and reimagining its traumatic bloodbaths day in and day out keeps the pall of death alive here.

Noted. Now let's dig deeper.

There is a superseding issue to all of this haunting business that never gets talked about and is the reason for much of the confusion. It's what I've been chiseling away at in this book to show not tell, but now I'll tell it: we don't know what we are.

When it comes to hauntings some people believe they know what they're interacting with. They have the certainty of a fool. Others admit they don't really know what it is that haunts or why. But where are the people who know the first order problem? Namely that we don't know what *we* are.

If it didn't before, does it now seem strange to you that we take for granted what we are and further take for granted that this version of self is capable of figuring out ghosts? Some go so far as to say we deserve to know anything and everything we set our minds to. But what if our minds are incomplete? Or worse, a festering illness? What if we are living in a set of delusions caused by a fugue state that began when we proclaimed ourselves divorced from, and hierarchically above, Nature?

We are born of and into Nature. Are our denials of this obvious fact not the equivalent of a child cupping hands over eyes and thinking mom and dad don't exist until the hands come down? Then and only then, there they are! Like self-centered magic!

The most rudimentary form our childish eye-covering takes is speaking about Nature as a "thing" and holding "it" at bay as best we can, outside of our house. A house made primarily of trees and metal alloys. In other words, a house made of Nature.

From there we devolve. We talk about God's will. We talk about being chosen or special in God's eyes. Or, if we're cleverer than the zealots, we assume we evolved out of Nature and then say we'll take it from here, thanks, because God doesn't exist, Nature is a lesser thing, and we might as well be gods. However, there's another word that better encapsulates arrogant people who strive for immortality, fancy themselves gods, and refuse the backwards gaze of a mirror: vampires.

We're a funny people, we postmodern whatever-we-call-ourselves-now. In all of our art forms, and in all of our bibles, we are in nonstop conversation with ourselves about good and evil. We tell ourselves what bad is, what monsters look like, how to avoid them and why. Then, in real life politics, we vote in the big bad whose mission is to sway us to identify with him by calling bad *good*.

Of course not all of us identify as political, which is itself a political identity. We shrug off politics as if we're unaffected, disaffected, or helpless. Some of us figure that the political system, comprised of and run by people like us, is out of anyone's control. We fancy that a rational conclusion.

What all of us are doing regardless of what we call it is making variations on the same political choices that provide consistency, even if that consistency is chaos. Complacency isn't as static as it feels. We are refreshing our choice to remain stuck in our thinking at all times. We're living in the shackles of free will, slaves on the plantation of super wealthy, super powerful elites whose wealth, power, and elitism exist by the grace of our social pacts. Perhaps Civil War ghosts stick around as invisible phenomena that periodically turn visible to remind us that we are at perpetual war within ourselves and therefore outwardly with each other.

There is no escaping this until we see the fact. Not for them. Not for us. To see a problem like this clearly is to no longer have the problem. Clarity is the death of a main problem and its satellite problems all at once. To that end, these ghosts have great purpose and meaning for our benefit even if they are unconscious of it. In turn, when their message breaks through and we get right with ourselves, we will benefit them. Currently, the Gettysburg ghosts have no future ancestors coming to set them free from their kuleana. But there can be. Our clarity is also their freedom.

Through the living, the dead are creating their escape. And neither of us know it.

Chapter 19
Bees: The OG Borg

Sunrise is busy time for the yard and beyond as day dwellers wake and call to their friends. Birds ask trees what they need today. Cows moo aloha in the distance. Listen intently and you may hear the neighing of a horse on the breeze. The breeze picking up into a wind that will shape the atmosphere. The atmosphere ringing with tinnitus-like tones.

Used to be busier. Used to be, prior to the 2018 Kilauea eruption in Leilani Estates, a time when the air sizzled with honey bees who lived in a hive right off the back porch. We never did see the hive, but it must have been nestled in one of the raised rock garden beds. Like a great engine rising from Earth we'd hear the hum faithfully when the sun first peeked over the Pacific blue. Where did the bees go?

I think they died in the eruption. When Madam Pele came home and turned on the lights, the sky turned to ash for much of the island. Carol and I were ridiculously fortunate in that we lived in a pocket where the ashy air blew around us, but we were directly affected for at least a week. In that week, the bees left. I don't think they got the memo and fled, I think they suffocated. But I don't really know, I just know that I miss them.

Yellow jackets and wasps also said their goodbyes. Listening to them rise from their tree nests and lava rock layers at sunrise from the gazebo was magical for sure.

Still, I didn't miss them as much. The yellow jackets eventually came back. The honey bees stayed gone until our new neighbors encouraged a hive in their yard. Now a new colony of bees are buzzing about and I'm thrilled.

I don't know what it is about bees that attracts me, besides the honey, but I've always loved them. They're colorful. They're dangerous but not a threat unless threatened, which makes sense. They're hard workers and their jobs are relatable.

Even as a child, it was easy to watch them and figure out some of what they were doing. When I was a wee lad I did just that. I don't remember where this field was, perhaps the lawn of my preschool, but I remember many a summer day spent lying in it on my belly to get my eyes as close to the bees as I could. We didn't have digital zoom on portable cameraphones back then. We had our observations, imaginations, and peppering questions for mom and dad.

I had a field of grass and dandelions. A field of bees pollinating flowers. And me, dumb as a stump, catching them in my hands, I had swelling. Getting stung was no fun. Crying was no fun. Doing it over again was pretty fun. I must have been a slow learner.

Looking back, I'm glad they weren't wasps.

***

I know I ended that last chapter all cool, like, *Boom! Mic drop! And we're out!* But we need to stay in magical Gettysburg for a spell if you don't mind. We will use it as a transition from talking exclusively about the dead to other invisible beings. If ever there is a place to discover a new liminal element to hauntings, it's Gettysburg. Here's one I've been sitting on for over a decade, unsure how to approach it until now.

My Paratopia podcast partner, Jeff Ritzmann, drove me to several notoriously haunted locations the handful of times we visited together. I want to tell you about two of them: Spangler's Spring, situated in Gettysburg National Military Park, and author Mark Nesbitt's Ghosts of Gettysburg Tour building on Baltimore Street.

Nighttime. Spooky. Me without a flashlight. This was the first time I visited Spangler's Spring with Jeff and a coterie of his family and friends. The Will of Silence almost immediately grew palpable in the body, wanting to exert itself. I let it spring into action and it briskly walked me to a line of trees quite a distance from our group, or any other tourists, in the black of night. Unbeknownst to me, Jeff was a bit worried that I'd taken off and gotten lost. The terrain was treacherous in places and I had no clue where I was going or why. I still don't. But I can tell you some of what the body did and how I felt while the Will of Silence was puppeteering it.

When I spontaneously arrived at what to me was a random destination, the Will of Silence performed a bunch of maneuvers with the arms and legs, most of which I don't remember now. Even if I did they would remain incomprehensible to me. I have no way to look them up.

The series of moves I do remember included walking me backwards in a circle over and over again. At some point The Will of Silence stopped that and began slapping my chest really hard. This produced a sensation of heat from the chest and in the environment all around. This was followed by a distinct phantom smell of gunpowder. Next, the Will of Silence had the hands gesticulate conversationally, or, dare I say, instructively, as if addressing a group of invisible people. I had the distinct impression of people all around me and the feeling that they were friends or at least friendly.

What I imagined was happening—and here I'm using the word "imagined" cautiously, which we'll come back to after you've forgotten about it—was that the Intelligence of Silence was speaking to ye olde ghosts in the grove. Both men and women. Perhaps it was telling them their kuleana was up and giving them permission to move on. Alternatively, it could have been imparting the knowledge that they were dead and explaining their choice to evaporate into a less stressful afterlife. I dunno. But after pantomiming that scene and hearing phantom laughter around me, I marched back to Jeff and the gang.

The second time I visited Spangler's Spring with Jeff and company, months later, it was again nighttime lit dimly by stars. And again me without a flashlight. I was trying to locate the exact stand of trees the Will of Silence had made such a big production in front of the last time. Couldn't find it, so I decided to allow the Will of Silence to do what, if anything, it wanted near some random trees away from people. I wouldn't want to be a ridiculous spectacle.

The energy didn't nag at me to come alive and do anything like the previous visit. I alone wanted to let it loose and see what happened next. The result was relatively unspectacular.

Oh, except for this one thing: what appeared to be a two-dimensional black shape similar to construction paper arrived out of nowhere. The shape, which appeared to be alive in some way, was about the size of an adult goose. It swooped jaggedly past me to my right, displaying the flight characteristics of a butterfly or a bat.

I thought maybe my eyes were playing tricks on me and it could be a bat, except it was too large.

Within minutes of this I noticed a pinprick of light either on the ground or hovering just above it over by some wood planks that I assumed covered a hole. I didn't know what the planks were for, and can currently find no information about them online, but we encountered them now and then walking around the battlefield. They were not the source of the light, though. In fact there was no visible source.

The Will of Silence walked me over to the dot of light. By the time I arrived it had disappeared. It then positioned me next to where the light had been and turned me around and around while looking up at the sky. The Will of Silence did this for a while, circling the body in place, me gawking at stars.

When it stopped it brought my eyes to the tree line. There was that black shape again, still big as a goose. It flapped its two-dimensional wings and swoop-fluttered around in front of me, putting on a little show before disappearing like a magic trick. That is to say, it did not fly away this time, it dematerialized. This startled me into blurting out to the darkness something elegant like, "What was that?!" The whole affair was jarring—most of all the fact that the flying shape seemed to be missing a dimension. I never saw anything like that before or since.

Oh, except this one time, later that first night, when Jeff and I brought a small group consisting of his family, a friend, and a couple of Paratopia listeners to Mark Nesbitt's notoriously haunted place of business, which included a bonus haunted upstairs apartment where he let guest speakers stay. We brought all of the usual ghost hunting accoutrement: cameras, handheld recorders, a laptop computer, open-minded people, skeptical people, and, in lieu of the obligatory psychic medium, experiencers who seemed to attract paranormal activity. This go-round we also brought two things different to the hunt: the Will of Silence and a theremin.

For those unfamiliar with the theremin, you know that spacey, high-pitched electronic whirring sound you hear in every 1950s UFO movie? That's a theremin. It's a musical instrument, the playable parts of which consist of two antennae. You don't touch them to play it. Instead, you hover your hands around them and they pick up and amplify your body's electrical current. You control the volume and pitch of the outputting tone by adjusting the proximity of your hands to the corresponding antenna. We wondered if ghosts might be able to interact with it. Why not? They can drain batteries and talk into voice recorders. Let's add theremins to the mix and see what happens!

Late evening into the night was fairly uneventful. But then, right on stereotypical cue, at around 3:00 a.m., all of the expected (if that's the right word) haunting activity amped up for about forty-five minutes and then died back down. In those minutes various of our crew heard children giggling in the room upstairs where child ghosts were said to reside. Heard phantom growling. Heard church bells ringing. Photographed what looked plainly like a ghost child, although the photographer, Jeff, didn't see anything when he snapped the shot. Had full batteries drain to zero in the cameras. Talked to the air and captured EVP responses. All the fun stuff you hope would happen happened, outside of a visible apparition floating through the halls. An apparition like "Hank," the Confederate soldier who haunted the green room downstairs.

The green room was where Mark Nesbitt did his book signings in the day. At night, it was an oppressive creepfest. An eerie thickness permeated the atmosphere of the room. Everyone in our group felt it. It caused a pressure on the chest that made it slightly hard to breathe. We set up a camera and an infrared illuminator there, and various of our people buddied up to record audio in the hopes of scoring an interview with ol' Hank.

No one felt comfortable being alone in the green room. Even so, I waited for everyone else to clear out so I could sit in it alone in the dark, save for the ambient light of a tabletop lamp in the next room. Just me on the floor near the entrance and the theremin, about four feet away, ready to communicate with the dead. We had an infrared camera trained on me. If some occult interaction were to take place, we'd catch it. I'd die, but we'd catch it.

I got comfy—as comfy as ostensible purgatory allowed—and asked if Hank, or whichever ghost may be in there with me, could prove his presence by triggering the theremin. With that question hanging in the room, I relented to the Will of Silence.

The Will of Silence began moving my arms and head around. It once again gesticulated my hands in ways that create power beyond my knowledge. My right hand sprung up and the palm flattened out to the side of my face, positioned evenly with my chin. My lungs pushed out a heavy sigh and then, eerily, the theremin came to life, clicking slowly at first, rising to a solid tone.

Of all the footage we recorded, this particular incident was the only one that disappeared. Mysteriously, of course. It was captured on mini digital videotape. Jeff and his wife, Lisa, watched it later. It vanished before I could scrutinize it.

Drat.

Jeff said that from their vantage point it looked as if the theremin was responding to me, not a ghost. They saw me do all those moves and then when I let out the big sigh, it looked like somehow, impossibly, that big breath triggered the theremin across the room. However, what I remember happening could not have been caught on camera, infrared or otherwise. It was perceptual and only available to me via the Will of Silence. What I experienced was this....

The green room smelled musty and old. There was already a thickness to the atmosphere, which became all the heavier the moment I gave over to the Will of Silence. In the far corner of the room to my right a self-contained blackness appeared to rise out of the floor and wall. It quickly floated over to me and hovered before my eyes, reminding me of the Smoke Monster from the TV show, *LOST*. I had the uncanny impression that it was evaluating me, sizing me up, so to speak. It felt like I was being judged by a massive black cloud entity who was comprised of many beings—a hive of minds living within a sentient hive. Something kooky like that.

My body moved all the while, hands a flurry of mysterious arrangements. The musty room stink was overtaken by a powerful scent of men's cologne, which was chased off by the smell of leather. This was not Hank the ghost, but perhaps Hank the ghost was this. Or, more boldly, perhaps Hank and all of the other ghosts here exist in one or more of these dark hive-mind beings and don't know it. Maybe it swallows souls and keeps them trapped in their memories, doomed to play out the same scenes over and over, which for this entity is like eating a fine meal where it can taste the individual ingredients. Or maybe when a cluster of people die unwittingly they form a disincarnate dust bunny that has its own unitary sense of aliveness, even while they retain something of their own identities, like a bunch of living humans unconsciously trapped in the sway of an archetype. Let's hope that one. When I popped my hand up by my face and let out the big sigh, this living, or perhaps undead, blackness took that as its cue to leave the way it came, through the corner of the room. That's when the theremin kicked in.

Mulling it over later I came to the conclusion that although this blackness didn't have wings or flutter-fly like the 2-D critter on the battlefield, it was the same being. An amorphous being of many beings. It is possible that I concluded wrongly, but one thing I know now for sure is that no one else in our groups saw such a being. I even asked listeners through the podcast if they had ever encountered anything like the creature(s) I described. No one said yes. And the reason is that I wasn't seeing with my eyes alone. I was seeing through the expanded awareness of the Will of Silence.

I won't go so far as to say that I was definitely seeing what ghosts are in their true form, but I highly suspect it. I suspect, that is, that there is a Secret of Silence to be found here: the Intelligence of Silence is one unbroken movement of clarity. Our separative minds translate this as different levels of clarity being applied to separate subjects, Therefore, when one looks through the eyes of the Will of Silence and sees with unbroken clarity, one sees more of what's there than even psychics pick up.

I saw more behind the veil but that doesn't mean I fully grasped the picture. It wasn't with my eyes that I was seeing, after all. Not even my so-called third eye. It was with the Will of Silence. The Intelligence of Silence grasps it. And the hive-like entity (or entities) haunting Gettysburg recognized this and wanted to check me out—but only after I yielded to Silence. It really had nothing to do with me, personally.

All of this explaining and hypothesizing and Mystery is leading to one final conclusion: we really don't know what we are. Not in this life. Certainly not dead.

In this life we're not even as alive as we could be. Given that, if I had been sitting in the green room alone in normal consciousness, would Hank or some other apparition have materialized? Did I see not the ghostly Confederate puppet but the puppet master behind him because I was running on the Will of Silence and not my own will?

Yes. I believe so.

And we want to pretend we've conquered death by hunting ghosts?

Come on.

Let's face it: familiar though the presentation of discarnate human voices and translucent human bodies is, when it comes to ghosts and hauntings, we don't know what we're looking at. And if we're not alive with the Will of Silence, we are completely blind to the potential hive intelligence deciding when, where, to whom, for how long, and why these presentations manifest.

Chapter 20
Bees: Like-Minded Mini-Mes

Of all the intriguing aspects of honey bee life perhaps the most fascinating has more to do with us than them. It's the disconnect between the fact that they are observably relatable and yet for all of our lives we've been told that most bees are basically organic robots. There's the queen who runs the hive, and then there are a kagillion male drones who do her dirty work. She's like the psychic center barking out orders to these dumb guys who are extensions of her. She has all the personality. They have none. Not an individual among them. As a kid this fascinated me, too.

I wish I had been taught to observe living beings with the clarity of my own senses, not through the fog of someone else's. Just a simple instruction not to ignore research, but to set it aside as I'm observing and relate what I'm seeing with what I've been told is the case, later. Perhaps then I would have come to know bees with the same undogmatic sobriety as I know ducks. It's hard to see past expectations set by years of research even when the findings were wrong.

In the case of bees, it turns out all of those observations were wrong. The drones aren't just drones, they are individuals. They have inner lives, emotional states, likes and dislikes, and longterm memories. Hive society is far more complex than a centralized mind distributed through multiple bodies with no personas of their own. Why would we get that so wrong for so long when we're all looking at the same bee people?

I'll bet it started with an initial refusal to see a complicated, relatable society in what we wanted to think of as "just bugs." Lesser creatures. Just insects making honey. Honey for us. Our prejudices always serve our selfishness. It wasn't merely easier to trust the initial observations and build on them with foggy vision, we thought it benefitted us to downplay their aliveness. Contrary, all truly benefit when we see clearly.

Thanks to our new neighbors, Carol and I may now watch the bees again, this time with clear eyes. I promise not to grab them. It takes time but even I can learn.

***

One of my favorite Willie Iaukea anecdotes comes from our mutual Hawaiian friend who named Imua. They were walking together down a dirt path in the jungles of Puna when suddenly Willie stopped in his tracks, stepped off the path, and stiffened up. He looked like he was averting eye contact with someone invisible. Our friend didn't know what was going on but she knew it was important to silently follow his lead without asking a barrage of questions. When Willie resumed as normal he told her that the spirit of a young Hawaiian man walked past. He was following the protocol his father had taught him when he was a young boy for encountering spirits.

Cool, right?

Not really. More like *culture*.

Having grown up an average White boy from Massachusetts I cannot imagine being taught respectful spirit encounter protocol. Issues such as those were not exactly kitchen table. More like living room. Specifically, on TV. More specifically, *The Twilight Zone.* Our culture didn't come from the land, it came from books and Hollywood.

Willie says the spirits he sees don't look vague or partial; they look like normal, solid humans walking around. The first inkling he gets that they are dead is by the garb they are wearing (or not wearing). And, of course, it helps when the person next to you sees no one strolling by.

Had I been with him that day would I have seen the spirit of a Hawaiian man walking the path? No, I don't think so.

Had I been with him that day with the Will of Silence active would I have seen a 2-D black shape the size of a goose fluttering where the spirit of a man walked? No, I don't think that, either.

I don't think spirits who were trained in life to remain conscious in death and roam Earth are the same as the ghosts of people who died with no preparation for that.

Here is my barely-informed, mostly intuitive, speculation about the afterlife: to continue existing as a ghost who haunts, a spirit who roams, a kernel of self who reincarnates, or a person who goes to a heaven or hell is to remain trapped in the stream of human consciousness. None of those situations are true death, for true death frees us from the currents of human consciousness. True death is the absence of the contents of consciousness, not their continuity.

The death of self is total liberation. For the average Westerner, death of the body while the self remains intact is as liberating as being transferred from prison lockdown to house arrest. If you're from a culture that understands something of the afterlife and knows how to consciously maneuver in it, however, you get to enjoy the perks of a prison guard. This is all crudely put but I need you to see the point.

Like a lucid dreamer who knows how to make conscious decisions while asleep, one may roam or reincarnate (depending on one's cultural training) in a self-aware manner. If one is unconscious, one just rolls with it. Maybe the unconscious soul reincarnates willy-nilly. Perhaps mom, dad, and Jesus wave them into the light. Or they fall into the deepest pit of despair to face their own demons. However formless awareness shakes out for them, they move through death in either a conscious or unconscious manner, as they did in life.

If that all makes sense, here comes the hard part: I don't think the person who lives an unconscious life may roam Earth unconsciously in death. The conscious soul is fully formed and aware to a much greater degree. That soul learned in life how and why to navigate death. The other type of person is at a disadvantage here. Believe it or not, this brings us back to Gettysburg with our 2-D shadow goose.

When you hear reports of ghosts roaming around spooking people, sometimes there is a bit of mischief in their antics, but more often they don't seem too conscious of their actions. Sometimes their appearance has synchronistic meaning for the people who encounter them, yet they don't appear to be timing their manifestations for such purpose. So who dies and becomes a ghost?

We have a pretty good sense of it from generations of anecdotal evidence, scant and controversial empirical evidence, folklore, and the movie cliches that have followed. Who becomes a ghost? Those who die suddenly, tragically, and feel like they have unfinished business.

Some alive people speculate that ghosts don't know they're dead. Others say that some do, some don't, and you can tell them apart by the specific type of hauntings. I'm going to posit something different. I'm going to say they all know they are dead and that's the problem. More to the point, the problem is that they were not raised to navigate death, likely because they didn't come from a culture where they were trained to stick around to guide family or to protect sacred locations.

From taking a bullet in a war, to running their car off a bridge, to being hacked to pieces by a murderous stalker, dying horribly in all its forms creates a common situation: in their final moment the victims of such circumstances end up being on such high alert as to pierce the illusion of autonomous self, the illusion of total control, displacing them into a state of hyper presence and hyper focus. And that state of mind is just conscious enough to preclude would-be helpers from bringing them anywhere, but not conscious enough to stay on Earth with purpose.

Let's pause here to recap the three death situations I am proposing, and who knows? Maybe I'll even come up with a good reason for having proposed them in the first place when what you really want is more ducks.....

Those who die self-aware with training and purpose for the afterlife know how to navigate with and within the invisible landscape. Easy peasy.

Those who die unconscious of what it takes to roam Earth while dead are met by guides, guardians, gods, or others who bring them somewhere. Alternatively, sorry to say, some will find themselves in a hell of their making. All in this category die into their cultural and personal expectations, or barring that, their unconscious wishes, which for some are actually fears based on guilt and shame.

Finally, those who should die unconscious like the second group, and not lucid like the first, are made lucid through reflexive response to the tragic circumstances in which they die. These people, who were trained in the lazy art of remaining an unconscious self—and who had prepared to hand over their afterlife to a god, a devil, an atheistically imagined nonexistence, or an agnostic shoulder shrug—are made hyperaware in their final moment. This creates a friction at death's door where they are neither totally unconscious and in need of transport nor totally conscious and sticking around to perform a duty. The friction gives rise to a Jungian lysis— in this case the emergence of a ghost-carrying overmind that comes into being as a self-organizing principle for the untrained, uninitiated people who are conscious enough to know they are dead but are bound to Earth without purpose. They are taken into the womb of this intelligence that they themselves have formed—a sub-archetype within the archetype of death—until they may be birthed into whatever is next.

Lacking the purpose of a cultural or occult collective, this intelligence gives them collective purpose, utilizing them like a puppet master to benefit the living. The manifestation of ghosts, at its baseline, tells the living that there is more to death than a physical ending. Deeper than that, for those who care to see that the stereotypes we have formed about ghosts and hauntings don't actually make sense, it hints at there being something else we cannot perceive behind hauntings and apparitions. Something we have blocked out with our own interpretations so that we may remain blind to reality, unconscious and incurious, having replaced genuine, innocent curiosity with an aptitude for indexing that has us reflexively categorizes what's being witnessed. Such categories are overwhelmingly based on erroneous research and experiencer supposition. It is from within this box of false knowledge that we wonder and speculate.

The dead, like the living, cannot see beyond the psyche. Such sight requires yielding control to the Intelligence of Silence, which transcends and includes the psyche. The Intelligence of Silence does not merely transcend and include the living and become the self-awareness of the living when the personal psyche dissolves, it also transcends and includes the dead. The Will of Silence, then, is the living force that runs on death energy. The Intelligence of Silence's formless, timeless action transitions and translates through the physical body via the dead, who exist betwixt and between form and formlessness, time and timelessness.

Ah, yes. Another Secret of Silence.

Though I am stating this authoritatively, I admit that the whole business of lysis overminds containing ghosts is speculation on my part. However, my speculation isn't just me out on a limb formulating another whacky idea to replace the whacky ideas we already have. My speculation is informed. Informed by similar examples in Nature. Informed by the existence of the Will of Silence in my life. Like recognizes like. Similarity, however, is not sameness. When we're talking about Nature we're talking about vital, primal living force. When we're talking about the Will of Silence we're talking about all of it: the living, the dead, and the awareness in which they manifest and operate.

My speculation is rooted in having lived 25 years and counting with a consciousness that transcends and includes normal awareness. A consciousness whose actions utilize the impeccable talents of dead masters from around the world. Ultimately, I speculate about the unconscious dead existing in and manifesting at the whims of a conscious bubble because I believe I have witnessed the bubble in the form of that living 2-D blackness. And I think its inner workings must be fractally the same as the inner workings of the Will of Silence, which are fractally the same as the inner workings of Nature.

Whether it's the intuition of ducks, the psychic mind of bees, inheritable ancestral talents and characteristics in human DNA, or the finding in physics that we are all one energy masquerading as separate objects, we cannot escape the fact that I is we is I. We are each other and to one degree or another we carry a spark of the people who came before us: the dead. It's undeniable and yet we rarely think of ourselves as the continuum species that we are. When we do we often laugh it off. "You must be high, man." But I is we is I and we have always known this.

Ducks don't neglect it. Why do we?

Chapter 21
Ms. Jackson If You're Haole

If you ever want to meet an alien dinosaur, check out the Jackson's chameleon sometime. Because it's not cool enough being lizards who change color to match their emotional state like a mood ring, these fellas have three horns like mini triceratops, long, thin tails that curl up into spirals, and fat, round eyes that dart every which way like Marty Feldman. Their toes spread out in crazy directions so that they can grip and climb pretty much anything, slowly. They move very slowly.

We have one living in the tree off the lanai. I see him now and again when I'm out there working. He's not my first, though. I had encountered them before when I lived in the small town of Kainaliu on the Kona side. I'd pick them up and let them climb me, which freaked out my roommates who swore they bite hard. Apparently they have large, sharp teeth, but I've not suffered a slow-motion chameleon attack to find out. I'm sure it happens if you ignore the signs that they don't want to play today. It reminds me of all the tales of vicious wild boar charging at you when the reality is they mainly want to make peace and sleep under a mango tree. Who doesn't love breakfast in bed?

A friend informed me that Jackson's chameleons came to the Big Island when some lunatic smuggled them here and set them free all over so that they would propagate. Looking it up online I see that a pet shop owner in Oahu had them shipped there legally in 1972, but they were all thin and sickly so he set them free in his yard. Strange story in that they are mostly found here on the Big Island, not so much on Oahu. The simple answer? Both stories are true. Someone had to have set a lot of them free here to have taken off the way they did.

It is telling how we have all of these stories of fear surrounding animals great and small ready to warn each other with and none of them are cautionary tales about how colonizing humans are the most violent, most invasive species of all. How many of our fears are projection? How many are our fault? Why do we laugh off the ending of every Nature documentary where the narrator says, "... Man."? I don't even have to explain that reference to you, do I?

I'll ask the chameleon next time I see him climbing away. He'll probably just look at me and several other things at the same time with that goofy grin he's got permanently etched on his face like a spinner dolphin.

Wait, is that him trying to slow-motion bite me?

***

The Intelligence of Silence has no opposite. It is the Ultimate Intelligence encompassing all intelligences. However, because I block it out as the sole first-person awareness of the body, I otherize it. And this is where I'm at with it: I am not living as The Intelligence of Silence, I am living in relationship with it. Hence, the Will of Silence behaves as if a separate entity cohabitating in the body with me.

Silence coming alive in the body took me by complete surprise. Creepily reiterated, there are two of us in here now: the Will of Silence and Jeremy. Perhaps for other people in this situation the friction of a half-hearted transformation conjures a lysis based on one's culture: a goddess, a serpent, a primordial creative impulse— whatever they have been told to unquestioningly know that the allegedly other energy is. I was never educated or interested in any of this, which is why, as I explained in chapter 14, I felt pressure to adopt the identity of another culture and live in that archetypal pattern. It never took hold.

Although I am creating a duality from the Will of Silence, my lack of definitions and explanations for it didn't prepackaged it for me. The upshot is, I can better see how this Will moves in the world than those experiencing a cultural cover story. However, my vision still may end up foggy if I'm not careful, for to walk in the expanded world that transcends and includes rationality is to walk a tightrope. Unverifiable and unexperienced stories of how it all works may appear in my mind fully-formed, and I may be tempted to shout to the world that I've figured it all out, as I warned about in my book, *I Am To Tell You This And I Am To Tell You It Is Fiction*. The title speaks to this.

The fact remains that we cannot see Nothing through a microscope. If the lens is strong enough, we will find illusory particles and indications of forces created by the act of looking. Likewise, we cannot see the prime forces behind beings and realms we occasionally witness or find ourselves in, and so the forces, or we, or both, may just do some world-building as a function of our looking. If we keep alert to this while we doggy paddle through the ocean of consciousness, perhaps we will avoid spinning in a whirlpool of validation and certainty about uncertain things.

Let me show you how this works.

I am certainly uncertain about there being an inky trickster creature in Gettysburg that has swallowed the lost souls creating it. The reason I feel comfortable throwing the idea out there is because it feels intuitively correct given how the Will of Silence works. It animates the living body with the expertise and precision of the dead who were masters of their craft in life. Also, with buddhas and other beings, perhaps even animals. As I detailed in *Urgency.*, when I began unleashing the Will of Silence on the regular, all sorts of interesting, "crazy" events took place. I hadn't thought about them this way when I wrote the book, but now I need to point out that part of what makes them crazy is their invisibility. To see the Will of Silence in action is to watch the body move around in esoteric ways while the *who*, *what*, and *why* remain invisible to the observer. I see more than that sometimes, but I don't see much more. And I highly doubt that if you were not alive in the same way and you were standing next to me you would see what I see.

So much of how we configure sanity is based on mutual observation and yet here I am, presumably sane. Sane enough to tie my shoes, write books, and hold conversations you won't want to speed walk away from so as not to upset the madman. Here I am living a life of high strangeness that is mostly unobservable to you and somewhat to me. For you to believe me about any of it requires that you trust I am sane, not lying, and not suffering an undiagnosed neurological disorder. For me it takes nothing to believe that another will moves the body when I shut up because it does. However, for me to believe me about the details of how that happens requires that I trust my own sense of inferences between the visible and invisible. This is easier to do in a one-to-one correlation, such as when the Will of Silence does partially familiar moves like acupressure, resulting in the alleviation of ailments, or completely foreign maneuvers that result in a change in the weather—both stemming from my ask.

If you are still reading this, odds are you have already granted that I am sane, not suffering a neurological problem, and you're really, really hoping I'm not lying. Lucky you, lucky both of us, I'm not. What I am is your microscope into the unseen world. And what's pulling into focus is I is we is I.

I look. I see multiplicity. That multiplicity exists within one consciousness, as do I. I, therefore, am that one consciousness. Until you hit this revelation for yourself in such a way that the body stops projecting *I* separate from all other *I's*, you've got me to examine the unseen for you. A flawed lens to be sure, but stronger than your microscope.

And what more do I see?

I see *I is we is I* everywhere and every way I look. And if I strain hard enough I see that this truth doesn't get realized in dead people any more or less than in living. You want continuity in death? It's the continuity of your being a lie.

I further see the differences between ghosts roaming around Earth, wondering what's up, and the spirits powering the Will of Silence. Here comes such a difference now....

As I reported in *Urgency.*, the very first time I meditated while sitting up in bed, a ball of white light about the size of a large marble floated into my bedroom through the closed window adjoining the back porch. It hovered in the air before me and then drifted back out through the glass. My impression was that it was a living energy mildly curious to see who had entered its field of perception. It saw me, was disinterested, and left the way it came.

I had seen other balls of light before. These were smaller and would appear to be dancing around in the corner of the room by the ceiling whenever I had marathon phone calls with friends. But this was the first time that a light ball came across as a thinking being.

Often, when just sitting in a meditative state, with that limitless energy enveloping the room I will see all sorts of energies in the atmosphere. Specks of black and white zipping around, and every now and then red. A white energy looking suspiciously like a fabric softener sheet also wafts in and out of perception periodically. Last night, I saw topaz blue glowing in our third cat, Gracie's, left ear for the first time. These energies don't strike me as alive, more like particulate in the ocean. If they are, they're about as alive as amoebas. I'm certain they serve functions but they aren't conscious the way the ball of light coming into the bedroom was, that's all.

Oh, I reported all sorts of neat stuff in *Urgency.*. Like the time I woke up some random morning and the Will of Silence wanted to come alive as I lay in bed. I didn't want that. I wanted to get up and start my day, and so I went to open my bedroom door. Wouldn't you know it, a phantom wind in the room blew the door closed. This wind, or force, blew the doorknob out of my hand a few times until I got the message that meditating was important and acquiesced. You will find what transpired in that book. It's not relevant here except to say that what I just described is an example of the Will of Silence itself acting in the room, beyond the body, to keep that door shut.

The Will of Silence allows me to see more of what's in the room, can interact with the room, and often implicitly states that there's much more I cannot see, which can only be the case if what I think of as the physical room is a limited conceptualization. Still, I haven't walked through any walls. Yet.

Not all intelligences are visible to me like that ball of light dipping in and out of the closed window. I've had many instances where it seemed as though the Will of Silence was bowing to someone and other instances where it was gesticulating as if talking to invisible people, just like it did in Gettysburg.

One time, back in Long Island City, New York, the Will of Silence spent a good long minute gesturing politely to what I intuitively knew was an invisible male human spirit standing right in front of me where my computer desk sat. Afterwards, I felt him move through me. The feeling was a cold chill, like a wind and a pressure moving through me front to back. It was not unlike what is often portrayed in horror movies when a ghost or a demon walks through a person. This definitely followed the lines of our fiction, though nothing horrible followed. Then again, those Hollywood writers have to study their subject to make their scripts feel authentic. Perhaps the fiction tropes come from real testimony. Or intuition. I don't know. I just know that the movie cliche is accurate. When someone walks through you, it's a wind, coldness, and pressure all at once, and you feel it moving into the body and out of the body.

My life hasn't all been invisible people in the room and visions in the mind's eye. I did once see a full-bodied apparition in broad daylight. This was back in high school, long before the Intelligence of Silence danced me around with its Will. Michael Jackson's music twirled me around back then.

My mother, sister, and I lived in the back apartment of a

small complex. Our front yard was the complex's backyard. We had a lanai-style porch leading to the front door at our kitchen. One fine day I was lying on my mom's bed with a bad stomachache. Her bedroom had two doors, one contiguous to the kitchen, kitty-cornered with the home's front door. Both of those doors were open. Only the screen door to the porch was closed.

I remember getting up to head into the kitchen when I was confronted by what looked like a vagrant reaching for the door handle. He was a White man with long, dirty, blonde or light-brown hair and matching beard. His face was dirty, as were his denim jacket and bluejeans. That one hand reaching for the door was grimy, too. Just a filthy guy. Sort of. Sort of a guy.

He had googly eyes. His pupils were bouncing every which way independently like a Jackson's chameleon. Seeing this dude about to break in, I reflexively screamed, which made me blink my eyes hard, and as quick as that he vanished.

My mom and sister were home. Mom came running to see what the problem was. I blurted out what happened and she stepped onto the porch, but, of course, didn't see anyone. I knew she wouldn't find the guy because the guy wasn't real. Or at least he wasn't materially real. Not only was he gone too quickly, he didn't make a sound. Not even the shuffling of running away. No shoe noise. No thighs rubbing together in those jeans.

Mom wasn't about to believe in ghosts so she assumed I was either hallucinating or that somebody had been there but had run away fast. Technically, it's possible I hallucinated him. I was feeling sick. I'd never hallucinated from a stomachache before, but it's as plausible as a ghost. And while I'm feeling charitable, the idea that there was a real man at the door who ran away also had the tinniest drop of merit. There had been another incident where I went to take the garbage out and found some teenager peeping in my sister's bedroom window in this little alleyway created by the tall, wooden fence of the adjoining property, a catechism school. I caught him and he ran away, making familiar clunky running noises of clothing rubbing against the fence and sneakers on concrete as he left.

The problem with that explanation is this: the physics of a lumbering vagrant with Cookie Monster eyes sprinting out of there quietly in the blink of a non-Muppet eye don't add up. He was just out. And yet the entire thrust of his movement had him about to open the screen door. I would think it would take a man a few startled seconds to react to me catching him mid-action and screaming. A few seconds for his addled brain to process that he'd been caught and choose which way to run and jump off the porch. He could bolt to his right to run down the drive or left to run down that alleyway, but not straight back because the yard was fenced in. All of his being startled and running and jumping would have to have been completely silent. What was he, a ninja duck?

A guy who is willing to bust into some stranger's house in daylight while people are obviously home is either on drugs or mentally ill. Why wouldn't he just let himself in anyway? Or touch the handle he was about to touch? Even accidentally brush it on his way to escape mode? Or let out a grunt of dissatisfaction before running? Maybe blurt out a swear?

Really, no answer involving a solid person made sense. And frankly, given my young life of high strangeness, and the fact that our apartment building was flanked by a Catholic church on one side and the church's catechism building on the other, I'm surprised we weren't swimming in undead salvation seekers 24/7.

If the dude was a ghost, is it not telling that I actually saw him, solid as Willie Iaukea sees spirits, as opposed to the invisible shenanigans I experience now through the Will of Silence? Would I see such a personification now or would I see a ball of light? Would I see a 2-D black mass swooping around? Would he be invisible to me altogether?

***

So that's some of the external stuff I've experienced that you might categorize as ghostly. Internally there is a different story being told. More like a series of them. There are the visions and recurring dreams that smack of encounters with lives being lived elsewhere in some etheric realm one may visit or engage with psychically. We've explored some of these. And then there's the story of the Will of Silence, which we will read now.

The main component pieces of this Will are the Intelligence of Silence and its actors. When the Intelligence of Silence speaks Truth either to you or as you, that is the direct voice of Ultimate Consciousness. This is why the wisdom shared is universal and absolute. When the Intelligence of Silence exerts its Will, however, its orders are not carried out through you or as you. They are carried out through the body by a flux of energy that contains multiple personas who are unalive experts, to put it bluntly.

There are outlier experiences to these. In one instance the Will of Silence adopted a frog-like persona. I don't know if it was a frog, a toad, or a conscious being who was like a frog or toad, but it maneuvered the body around my bedroom in Queens like a frog, squatting down and sort of hopping about the floor a little bit while moving my mouth around in absurd ways. As comical, or perhaps mentally ill, as that may sound, I wouldn't be surprised to learn that these were exercises which mimic the behavior of frogs to some healthful ends. Many are the contorted, animalistic faces the Will of Silence has made, only for me to stumble upon an obscure video of some Buddhist monk doing the same facial gymnastics as a form of yoga.

Speaking of Buddhists, let's talk buddhas. A couple of times, not many at all, just a couple, quite distinct buddha entities came alive in this here body. When that happens the eyes go wide and there's almost a palpable halo around the head. I feel like the body is exuding light into the room and there's a feeling of great, vast contentment to it that is indescribable. In that moment, I know what the Will of Silence is: it is both me and not me. In that moment, one of the main questions of this book and my life is answered: one does not experience the full emersion with all of these entities and personas—these experts and buddhas—so long as one remains a separate self experiencing the Intelligence of Silence as a parallel living force. My need for another death of self lives on.

Since I am still here, sustained by doubt, I might as well tell you about the non-buddha experts floating in the proverbial faucet, waiting for me to turn on the still proverbial tap. One whom I perceived to be male was the primary force throughout my New York years. He was distinct because he walked the body around with a bad limp. A limp like my right leg was dragging a ball and chain. This persona would do yogic exercises, including trying to get me to do handstands, whirling dervish twirls, all kinds of neat acrobatics. One thing I could never figure out was when he would center one foot like a compass and drag the other leg around in a circle over and over, and then walk a straight line through it between two walls of the room. It seemed as though he was trying to create something in the room, but I never perceived what. Sometimes he would touch my forehead to the wall and spin the body around with my forehead pressed against it as best he could. Alternatively, he would sometimes press an index finger to the wall and spin the body around. Maybe he got preoccupied with that game and never finished the creepy portal or whatever he was building.

I do remember several times when this, shall we say, artistic endeavor was in full swing, feeling as though I was being watched from the next room by an invisible someone whose presence caused a rising fear great enough that I called it quits in those moments.

Sometimes the line between bravery and stupidity is knowing when to leave a fearful situation, not ignore it or conquer it. Or so I tell myself.

And there are other personas, not just Limpy Limperton. Not all male. In fact more than one of the buddhas was female.

Whenever I ask any of these entities, who they are or what they are, I get the same answer that I receive when I genuinely thank them or am in a state of thankfulness with them, which is this weak, almost under the breath, expulsion of melting laughter that you might hear from someone who is deaf or mentally challenged. It's a genuine, good-natured laugh by someone who doesn't know how.

That's as close as I've gotten to a vocalization as none have ever spoken to me. Not even in my mind. So they're not entities in that way. They are not channeled.

They don't have a message to impart. And they are not possessing me.

Like raindrops comprising a body of water, they are the forces that comprise the energy that powers the movements of the Will of Silence. They constitute a liminal buffer between timelessness and time, formlessness and form, and they surface in accordance to either what I request, such as rain or healing, or what I need, which I may be unaware of, but is in more urgent need of attention.

The point of *I is we is I* is the same as *I am the universe and the universe is me.* I am not only all of we, humanity, but also all of we, the universe. We, the beings in Nature. We, the dead. I am all because I transcend and include all.

My original face is your original face: I am Nothing. You are Nothing. Everything is Nothing. Everyone is Nothing. That is our deepest impersonal situation. However, the shallow personal situation is being a walking, talking mask over this. That mask does feel fear. I feel it; you feel it, too.

Oneness containing multiples is as scary as the foundation of all that exists, which is to say, not at all. Nevertheless, when I, the mask, gaze into the depths that I cover, I experience burps of fear that are fleeting and not predictive of vomitous outcomes.

Yup, I just wrote that.

The point is, only people wearing masks of false autonomy make a horror show of what's natural. We call them Halloween masks. And, uh, a lot of people are wearing them. Like, most of us.

So, we've got a real problem here.

Chapter 22
The Secret Door

Of the myriad au naturel pest control options available, ranging from orange sprays to diatomaceous earth powder, I find the one that works best for longest in the garden and on trees is neem oil. Supposedly, spraying a mixture of neem oil and water on seedlings and roots will teach the plant how to fight against bugs from the inside out. All I can tell you is I planted kale, mustard greens, parsley, and red cabbage seeds directly into the ground and sprayed the dirt with neem. When seedlings began growing I sprayed their leaves twice more. Haven't had a bug issue yet, including Hawaii's dreaded nematodes. Finally, a successful garden!

To be fair, I also planted a bunch of cilantro, dill, and green onion around the aforementioned crops. Critters don't much care for their smells. And sweet potato was still going strong from last year's harvest. I consider that a diversionary plant for bugs to chew on. That all must help, too.

Still, it is for reasons all good that neem oil has an excellent reputation as the go-to for bug control. And so you might think that a neem tree, which produces the drupes and seeds that become neem oil, would act as kryptonite to the critters of the world. Nope. We have one in the backyard. Inside the duck run, in fact. It's crawling with ants. Small birds build nests in its branches. Heck, a banyan tree attempted to overtake it until I put a stop to that. At least twice a year either some sort of rodent or a mongoose burrows into its root system. I've never seen who it is, but I dutifully plug up their secret doors with rocks, lest the ducks throw an unstoppable quacking fit. And that takes care of that until the next tree squatter moseys along and tries to set up a ducky basement butcher shop.

Clearly, the neem tree does not heed the advice of its own oil.

Hypocrite.

***

Neem trees aren't the only people with secret doors at the base of their spines, we have them too. Also full of life. Or death. However spirit beings are categorized.

No, I'm not talking about the spot where the Will of Silence originally comes alive, I'm talking about an ethereal slit that opens and closes. A slit that breathes in energies and beings and breathes you out of the body and into Nothing. Nothing, which is manifesting everything within universal consciousness. I'm talking about where the Will of Silence is leading, which I breezed past in chapter 14 because neither of us were ready for this conversation.

Now that I've laid the groundwork, we're ready. Ready to talk about the Secret of Silence so secret you've never heard anyone whisper it until I opened my big fat mouth and wouldn't shut up about it through the oughts. All of the Will of Silence activity we have been exploring, including the universe's response to Silence, has been leading to this secret: There is a door in your spine, and you're not the one who opens it.

***

A door in the spine. A Secret of Silence so secret that it is guarded. Thus far I have had this door opened three times in my life. All three took place in bed, in early morning, but I was not asleep in any instance. The first two times happened after I had awakened and was lying on my back thinking about starting my day. The third happened while lying on my left side, shortly after climbing back into bed from having used the bathroom. Let's take them in order and see if we can't spot differences between this Secret of Silence and the noise of imitation. Incidentally, we'll also be spotting why that shroom chapter was so detailed.

The first instance took place about a month after my recurring dreams of being led through a 5-star spa & retreat in hell died down. It was basic as far as these things go. I was lying in bed, contemplating prying myself up, when I felt a hairline slit open in my lower back. It didn't hurt. It felt like the numb pressure you feel when a doctor uses a scalpel on your skin after having anesthetized the area.

The slit "cut" open upward, I'd guess, two or three inches in length along my spine. Immediately, a beading, blissful energy poured into my back from the slit. It vibrated all throughout my backside from head to toe—but only my backside. It felt like I was levitating on energetic pingpong balls of relaxation and joy. They were palpable balls, or beads, of manic, kinetic, felt energy. I don't know how else to describe that except to say I felt great physically and mentally for however long this took place. Sixty seconds, maybe? Less?

When time was up the rapid-fire balls of energy emptied out through the slit and I felt the slit zip back down. I didn't control it. My nervous system went back to normal, as did my mental state. This event didn't heal my slipped disks back to 100% or anything miraculous like that. It just felt next-level amazing in the moment.

The second instance, which took place a couple of weeks later, began much the same way: lying in bed, lying on my back, contemplating what I wanted to do with my day. Slit opened up and in poured the blissful balls of kinetic energy. Filled me head to toe, but only my backside, and then a new wrinkle: our demon-looking friend from chapter 14 slid in with it. The same demon, I believe, whose likeness canvassed the wall of the hell spa yoga center.

As possessive forces go, this fella didn't feel evil. He looked the part, though. I could see him superimposed over my flesh. He had muddy red skin and claws. I could see his jaw as he made my teeth gnash. However, I could also feel something of his interior experience and he didn't feel menacing. He felt ancient and immensely powerful, whatever that equates to. I had the vague sense that he was, in fact, a male who originated from a desert land. And, to steal what I wrote in *Urgency.*, he was basking in the glow of being alive for the few seconds he had in this here body. Fifteen seconds, I'd estimate. He was grateful for a fifteen-second vacation. I was grateful it wasn't a staycation.

Fifteen seconds up, the beading bliss energy poured back out through the slit, Mr. Demon with it, and the slit zipped down. The rest of my day was fairly uneventful, thanks for asking.

The third and thus far final time this slit opened took place between 4:00 a.m. and 6:00 a.m.. I don't recall how long after the first two episodes this occurred, but I did jot down that it happened on Thursday, March 25, 2004. I went to bed around 4:00 a.m.. At some point between 5:30 a.m. and 6:00 a.m. I got up to pee. After I stumbled back into bed, I couldn't get comfortable. I had a headache and was restless. I finally settled on my left side facing the wall, when suddenly the slit in my back opened up. Same deal as the previous two times in terms of the beading energy pouring in. No demon this time. This time there was a white light behind my eyelids and I had a sense that there were people standing behind me in the room. I didn't open my eyes and roll over to check it out because I didn't know how literally to take the feeling of surgical precision to the slit opening and closing. I didn't want to screw up the surgery, if that's what this was.

I didn't have too terribly long to contemplate this because in short order, the energy breathed out the slit and I breathed out with it. I wrote about this in *Urgency.* and won't bore longtime readers with it again for at least another 5 pages. The thumbnail is, we're all "God." Surprise! And what that looks like is Nothing being. What's Nothing being? Everything.

I experienced pure awareness exploding the universe into existence and then took on all first-person perspectives of the stuff of the universe at one time, including Spirit riding through the universe with the glee and exhilaration of an unafraid child on a rollercoaster. For Spirit, the universe is literally the theme park of mind —and we are all Spirit, all the universe, all the ride. This is why I am certain that you literally are the universe and the universe is literally you. It's lived experience. Yours waiting to happen. Hope you like rollercoasters.

Alright. So. I had this experience.

No, I *was and am* this experience, which ended with a lame contactee-style message from the faceless female voice I knew from abductions. Accompanying Her was a chorus of voices repeating a personal-to-me psychic prediction that soon came true. I concentrated on the headache I'd gone to bed with. Doing so pulled me back into my body. I entered through the slit and floated my way to my head. Saw my own blood and guts along the way—it was quite the jaunt. Slit closed and I leaped out of bed.

There were no people in the room that I could see. No bright, white light. Just me pacing like a caged tiger, and wrestling with the unspoken yet deeply felt choice before me: stay normal with this as an experience in my rearview, or forever be that alive. Who ya gonna be, Jer?

Whether the choice was real or not I cannot say. It's possible that the return to normal is a return to confusion, false choices, and the illusion of control, which immediately congeal into the appearance of an offer. But in the moment it felt real, it still does, and I chose to be me. I felt the need to share what had happened with anyone who would listen because I knew that state was a glimpse of human wholeness for all, not just some amazing thing that happened to me. Universal aliveness is—capitalization here we come—true Human Nature, not the bumbling mass of egoically partitioned morons running around screwing things up that we pretend to be. We need to know what we need to be and, ironically, I didn't know if I would be able to communicate it if I were living in true Human Nature mode.

Can a moth convince inchworms that not only are they the same being, the inchworms must become moths or eventually go extinct? I mean do they even speak the same language to have such a conversation? How does one walk through duality with nondual vision and act normal?

I dunno. I didn't know then, either. So here I am. Me. With all of these juicy "more real than real" experiences to compare with other so-called peak experiences that we are told are all the same. Let's look at that, shall we?

Since the allegedly more real than real mushroom trip is my most vivid example of what is taken for a spiritually enlightening experience these days, let's work with it. Superficially, it has much in common with the I AM universe-arising-from-awareness-arising-from-Nothing experience, but one is Silence and the other is noise. One transcends and includes the universe; the other originates within the universe. One is timelessly the case that you and I are when the self of psychological time is no more; the other takes from this and creates experiences for you to have in time. These experiences may lead you to believe you've left time behind when what has vanished is your perception of time. The universe doing this is not much different than how your body takes events from your waking life, as well as the collective, and repurposes them in a fluid form we call, *dreams*.

Dreams don't have to play by the rules of physics or time or even selfhood. How they unfold often doesn't make sense when you ponder them later, and yet a sense of internal logic persists within the dreams themselves. The way dreams play fast and loose with the rules of perception leads many a person to conclude that all dreams are more real than what we perceive after the alarm goes off. Some are; most aren't. However, as with the psychedelic trip, we confuse the dropping away of our perception of time in dreams with it having actually dropped away. Since your body is still aging through all of those experiences, and since you are an aspect of the body, it's safe to say you're still in time.

Recall that you are brain cells, are thought. Thought experiencing the rules bending, breaking, and disappearing, virtually, because that is as close to Nothing, to Truth, to timeless nonduality, as thought may get.

Although it steals from Truth to create its art, the mushroom trip has more in common with not only dreams but psychosis as well. Of course it does; they are both restless expressions of a disorderly mind. A mind that desperately wants to incorporate Truth's order within itself. Yet how can the limited incorporate the unlimited within it? It can't. It can only fool itself into doing so because the actual requirement is its death. Such a mind does not want death, just death benefits.

You wouldn't be inclined to notice that there is any difference, a chasm of a difference, between entering other states of mind and the absence of mind unless you've died egoically while the body remained alive. When I go on about being possessed by an ancient being and becoming the universe from Nothing? Probably sounds to you like I might as well have been high. Like there are distinctions without difference. But the difference is the difference between waking up for real and "waking" into another dream that cleverly has you believing you've woken up. Ever do that?

You're doing it now. But no more. Let's send in the clown one final time....

The idea that, while on shrooms, I became a cartoonish, animalistic clown mocking my own emotional reactions moment to moment is a bit too on the clown nose of who I am normally to really be a creature from another dimension either inhabiting me or revealing its interconnected existence with me. The external portions of the shroom trip were very much like dream materials spilling into the room to redefine waking reality. That included me. There was no carney barker mushroom entity speaking through me, that was me. There was no clown person I morphed into, that was me. This was a shallow representation of I is we is I. The "we" here was a splintering of egoic "I." It was dissociation, not transcendence or possession.

I may choose to examine what I was telling myself about me by putting on those voices and costumes. Psychological discovery and healing are recurring themes of all psychedelic experiences that I am aware of—at least for Westernized people. Same with dreams. However, this is a far cry different than being temporarily inhabited by an actual being.

The actual being I was inhabited by, that demon-ish person from another realm, had a backstory. Had an inner life. Had a sense of what it was to be him—and I could feel him. Whatever purpose he may have had for me, he also had his own purpose. He wasn't there to help me figure out my personal psychology. He wasn't there to quell my fear that I was going crazy while propelling me along into scenario after scenario until the chemicals ran their course. He was there to bask in the glow of being alive in this body for the brief window he had, and that's it. To that extent, it was selfish of him. Not in a bad way, but he got something out of it. Got something out of it because he wasn't a figment of my imagination or that of the collective being dreamed into the room by fungi or brain chemicals.

I was shown around a building where this being was worshipped through recurring dreams that weren't regular dreams and yet I felt that his origin was a desert land. Maybe he wasn't a demon but a lizard person. His skin tone and scaliness track with that.

I know reptilians have become a trope of alien abduction claims in recent decades. I know that an English sportscaster who once claimed to be Jesus incarnate, David Icke, popularized the notion of reptilian shapeshifters. And I know that *reptilian people* was originally antisemitic code for *Jewish people*, which may or may not have been what David Icke meant—Who knows with that guy? But I don't believe in reptilian aliens. I don't believe in anything David icke has to say. I am not antisemitic. I'm just telling you what I experienced. The being that inhabited me wasn't any of these. He wasn't a Sleestak from the *Land of The Lost* TV show, either, come to think of it. And seeing his form superimposed over mine while being "possessed" by him wasn't the same as what I experienced on shrooms. On shrooms, my physical appearance became someone else's. My apartment took on the solid appearance of another place. None of it looked superimposed. Similarities are not sameness.

This isn't the only similarity between experiences of Silence and experiences of high fidelity noise, though, is it? Let's scrutinize the fact of multiple perspectives happening at once from a different angle. Again, in the shroom trip this takes the form of splintered personalities. In the universal I AM experience it is clear that the self-identity of the universe is you and me when we're not pretending to be you and me. When we're really awake, in other words, not dreaming that we are.

What do you look like when you're not dreaming of your own autonomy?

Everything.

You, as universal consciousness, are multiplicity. You are the hot rock jettisoning through space. You are the stars and the planets they give life to. You are the life of those planets. You are Spirit whipping through it all like a smiling wind. You are the formless consciousness giving rise to these forms and activities. These aren't splintered personalities pretending to be different than the person emoting them, these are the fact of oneness being twoness by simply being. It's not a cheap psilocybin knockoff, it's the actual.

Another way to spot the difference between multiplicity being the case of universal consciousness and the shroom trip faking it is to consider that on shrooms I experienced myself as a pipsqueak of a voice in the back of my own mind while collective mind was spilling into and reshaping the room. Concurrently, I was still the one making decisions such as getting up and moving about. It was like a video game in that way where I was the player with the controller pressing the buttons and moving the joystick who would direct where the clown character went. I thought at the time I was a small, helpless voice, when in reality I was still controlling the body.

In the universal I AM experience I had a sense of washing out of the body through the slit, then blank. Nothingness. Next, formless consciousness and also me. Also me worried that I'm suffering an aneurism. Me feeling the formless consciousness that I am stretching in the brain that I just left. Me feeling it snap and seeing a light that I also am. And from that light, the universe exploding into existence, and I am that. Now I'm no longer Jeremy worried about dying, I am all of the universe living. This includes Spirit enjoying the ride.

I, Spirit, have an interiority. I know what it feels like to be me: unbridled joy. Not tickle torture, but true, unmatched exhilaration in being everywhere, being all moments in one moment. Not stagnantly all over the place like a fog, but dynamically moving, like life itself. And this includes a particular star that in duality, in time, is a future life I may or may not attaint depending on who I am when I die. But here in the now, it already is me. It can never not be me. And I am giving life to a planet in a coordinated effort with all other stars in the universe. It takes a village.

Jeremy is not here controlling this timeless moment. This timeless moment is here when Jeremy is not. It is only when the plurality pulls back into one focus that Jeremy exists again. That's when I'm hovering in space, staring at a planet, listening to a message from Her, and scheming to get back into my body by concentrating on the headache I'd gone to bed with. Jeremy is a thought construct and so Jeremy is always in touch with his brain. By identifying with my body through that pain, I am able to swim back into it through the slit and regain normal singular awareness.

Compare that again with the magic of mushrooms. That trip refused to end until the substance had run its course through my system. Heck, I couldn't even fall asleep and ignore it. It was fatiguing. Being the universe wasn't fatiguing, it was natural. It was a taste of how we are supposed to express and experience our lives when we drop the false human nature act. It was and is real.

And yet... and yet... here is this unreal thought construct who was named "Jeremy" by his unreal parents living unreal lives in an unreal society on a really real world. And Jeremy knows that his natural state as multiplicity is an affront to his false sense of sovereignty. He wants to exist even though he is a phantasm, just like in dreams. Every time he gets involved it is at the level of self-preservation in the face of the unknowable. Knowing this and understanding logically that his interference is a wrong move never stops him from making it. It's reflexive. He is reflexive.

His existence is the reaction that blocks out right action. He's the chaotic noise of modern disorder that demands its own existence over both Silence's and Nature's implicit order. If he had only done mushrooms and not also died into all of our true identity years before, he might tell you how enlightened they made him. But he has been All. And all he can rightly tell you is how enlightened none of us are. How no experience makes one enlightened. How that movie MacGuffin we all search for to claim to be enlightened or have enlightenment isn't contained in an experience. It either is you or it is not.

It is not. Not you. Not him.

Ducks? Well, ducks. They're another story.

Worth noting, too, is the difference in internal/external experience between mushroom trip and the authentic. As I explained in chapter 8, with eyes open, my environment on shrooms became that of a rubbery jungle. Door frames were off-kilter. Shadows moved and became friends or enemies. Random, weird scenarios happened to the room and to me. And with eyes closed, I was astrally jetting off to far away worlds, "spiritual" planes, and into the intelligent fog of a Hindu god. So much novelty was crammed into those nine hours, it's impossible to remember most of what happened.

With the door along my spine, although it's likely invisible (I can't see back there to verify), it does not feel internal. It feels like an organ of the body located on the surface of the skin. The feeling of people in the room that third time also felt external.

The first time the door opened, it felt like that energy was pouring into my physical body from some other place by way of interiority. I mean, even though the slit felt physical and external, the energy coming in didn't feel like it was coming into me from the air. Neither did the "demon" in the second opening, who, let's remember, was both internal and external. I could literally see his flesh superimposed over my own and I could also feel what he was feeling and gather a little information about him. The third time, the universal I AM experience, had me being washed out the slit and into Nothing giving life to the universe as me. There is no experience in the wilds of the mushroom trip that can compare to this—to literally seeing through the "eyes" of all so-called objects, and Spirit, and wind, and flora, and sentient stars, at once. I dragged myself back from this by concentrating on a pre-existing physical pain in my head. When I did, I floated through my own internal organs, both an external witness to them and literally inside of myself. This is a far cry from an internally-generated event or realm, and a far cry from uncontrollably being jettisoned into astral scenario after astral scenario.

Let's not overlook the fact that the slit opening those three times came in a sequence. First, basic energy. Next, basic energy and this other being, perhaps for purposes of me facing the demon. Finally, universal consciousness. It was intelligently sequenced by someone to, at the very least, acclimate me to this door. And the sequence happened only after I had gone through the death and resurrection of self, now with the Will of Silence, which subsequently awakened me to the reality of psychic abilities for clarity's sake. I would argue that my not getting attached to them is what propelled me to the point of readiness for those door-opening events. Tests, all along the way.

Mushroom trip?

No tests. No discernible sequencing.

But it's hard to see the totality because you make it hard. You don't want to end, you want to add on. Be better. Feel better. As is.

And so speaking Silence doesn't just kill it because it is timeless and we're speaking timelessness into time, it also kills it by warping the meaning through translation. Translation based on personal perspective, which is usually corrupted by desires both conscious and unconscious.

We really do a number on Silence, let me tell you! We simply won't shut up about it. Until we do, we are lost. Lost on a time scale of long cycles churning out interconnecting natural cultures that deteriorate into unnatural, selfish cultures who would rather commit murder/suicide, so long as they feel like they are in control, than die internally to absolute order.

To quote *Her*: "I understand hither/thither, and in that understanding shall neither be swept away nor carried on the seas of time." She interrupted a dream to tell me that. Looking it up online led me to the answer to a personal question, as detailed in *Urgency.*. Now, revisiting it on its own, not anxiously searching for an answer to the riddle, I see what was always true: the riddle is the answer.

The question is, will you continue to be either swept away or carried by time's strong forces? Or will you understand the dilemma? Understand spacetime, the very physics of the universe, and therefore you?

Not in any complicated way that takes a high IQ and specialized education, but in the way it was intended: as an adult with the innocence of a child. By asking, not answering, because you're intensely curious and guileless, not fearful and controlling.

Are you open to ultimate transcendental death? Or just the promise of a new-and-improved resurrected you?

Sit with this. Ponder it as the sirens of our collective murder/suicide blare in the background. Be free to do that. Free, ultimately, to do nothing.

Who awaits us in human wholeness?

What secrets reveal themselves then?

What if the secret door has a secret of its own to share, but only when one is ready?

What if the slit is not a door at all for such a one?

What if it's a gill?

Caramel & White

After a long while of doing meaningful gestures in the air, yogic poses, purposeful self-flagellation, and pressure-point energy movements along Caramel & White's spine, this body, "my" body, walked the circumference of her duck pen, hands flailing at intervals along the way. It reminded me of the manner in which the hands moved as I was led through that meditation retreat in dream hell. There, they were working the environment for my protection and fortification. Here, it was for her.

The Will of Silence stopped me at the precious duck in the pool. This body squatted next to her and repeated an opening of the hands motion as if to say, "Fly! Be free!" over and over again. It was like the Will of Silence was opening an invisible *Book of Life and Death* for her to choose. Choose to let go. This was not my intention.

As I've impressed upon you throughout our time together, the Will of Silence doesn't perform the random movements, tics, and gestures you may find people with large online communities who know more than I alleging. It moves the body with discipline and purpose—always with purpose. In many cases, like this one, it moves the body in sets of actions.

In the case of Caramel & White, there were seven sets of action involved. The first set of movements prepared this body and the environment around us for set two. Set two entailed reading and influencing the energy around and within her from a distance. Set three was a combination of hands-on pressure point therapy and associated motility in the air above her. Set four, the Will of Silence had me take a few steps back, gesturing and dancing about in yogic poses.

I surveyed the other ducks standing by her outside the run. I surveyed Caramel & White. The connection between us had deepened by this set. I inhaled and held it for a long time while dancing on the grass, then released it.

Having expelled most of the oxygen from my lungs, I stopped breathing again while staring at her. Staring through her. Staring into her. Merging with her on some level in that moment. And then staring with her. At that, I took in another deep breath through the nose.

Set five, I walked the circumference of the poultry netting, bent down, and stared at her again. Then I stood and walked around gesturing a bit. I inhaled and struggled to exhale. My breathing was heavy and shallow. My breathing was not mine alone. My breathing was hers.

I burst into tears. Deep tears from the gut. My gut started palpitating like often happens with a good cry. Unlike that, this was not spontaneous. Here, I felt myself purposely zeroing in on a place in the stomach where I physically held my attachment to Caramel & White, and I expelled it. Rather, the Will of Silence expelled it. I was just there witnessing all of this. I was going through it and going through the motions of it at the same time.

The sixth set of movements was mental. I realized that I was wrong. I was not helping to heal her like I had imagined. I was helping her to move on. There was a ritualistic quality to some of the gestures and prancing about that I had been performing. I now understood that I had been preparing the way for her, or something to that effect, to ease her transition into death.

I felt deep sadness, yet my sadness was not just my sadness. My sadness was her sadness. My sadness was life's sadness at its end through her.

Like ducks and everyone else, you and I carry death wherever we go. We are destined to die and so we are already dead. We have already died, we just don't know when. Even so, there is always sadness and grief in death. One must ultimately let that go. Let go the attachment. One must do so because it, like death, is inevitably there.

The seventh and final set of movements was both physical and mental. I said my goodbyes. I spoke my apologies. I told her I loved her. I walked back to the house a bit numbed out.

The seventh set did not involve the Will of Silence. The seventh set was all me.

***

Caramel & White might not have understood all of what my movements were for, but neither did I. Like me, she understood their core. She understood Love. I know this because of the way she said her goodbyes. I found her nestled beneath the neem tree, dead and hardened in her favorite spot to give birth. I had already taken away the quarantine cage she slept in to clean it, and now a large branch had fallen on the exact spot where the cage had sat. It was as if she snapped it off on her first and final flight, an obvious sign for me to find and know it was her posthumous goodbye.

No, not as if that, it *was* that.

I buried her body in lava rock near the gazebo. Later, out there in the aloneness, The Will of Silence danced a healing dance for the living.

This book is dedicated to Penelope who passed away during its writing. We love you, Penelope. You were such a kind and beautiful duck.

Special Thanks

Tyler Kokjohn for being my editing hero. Your suggestions made this a much better book.

John Randall for swooping in at the nth hour with fantastic cover art. You captured them perfectly.

Carol Fong for herself, ducks, cats, the sanctuary, the gazebo, and, oh, everything else, no biggie. I love you.

And Hawaii. Mahalo for the warm welcome at every turn. Without you I wouldn't have written anything like this book.

The Goonies don't need special thanks. They get it.